DEATH
ON DELIVERY

DEATH ON DELIVERY

The Impact of the Arms Trade on the Third World

CAMPAIGN AGAINST ARMS TRADE

First published in Great Britain in 1989 by
Campaign Against Arms Trade
11 Goodwin Street,
London N4 3HQ.

Written and researched by Helen Collinson

Designed by Mick Keates, London
Typeset by Florencetype Limited, Weston-super-Mare
Printed by Blackrose Press, London

Cover photograph by Mike Goldwater (Network).
Permission sought for cover photograph of man holding rocket
launcher but photographer not traced.

British Library Cataloguing in Publication Data
Collinson, Helen, *1962–*
    Death on delivery: the impact of the arms trade on
    · the Third World.
    1. Military equipment. Foreign trade between
    developing countries & developed countries
    I. Title   II. Campaign Against Arms Trade
    382'.456234

    ISBN 0-9506922-4-7

CONTENTS

CAMPAIGN AGAINST ARMS TRADE works for an end to the international trade in arms (starting with an end to all British arms sales) and for the conversion of military industry to socially useful production. CAAT provides a wide range of educational and campaigning materials including leaflets, briefing papers, pamphlets, and a slide/tape show. The Campaign also has a national network of local representatives and speakers. If you would like to learn more about CAAT's work, contact:

CAAT, 11 Goodwin St., London N4 3HQ (01–281 0297).

INTRODUCTION

Historically there has always been an arms business, but never before has the production and sale of weapons so shaped the world economy as today. Since the end of the Second World War, the international trade in so-called 'conventional' or non-nuclear weapons has undergone a world-wide boom. Arms sales have become synonomous with big business and single deals worth billions of pounds are not uncommon nowadays.

The sellers in this market are primarily industrialised countries in the North (such as Britain)[1], while most of the buyers are in the less-industrialised South, broadly deflned in this study as the Third World.[2] Although there is a considerable amount of illegal and private arms dealing going on around the world, the bulk of the arms trade consists of legal [3] transfers between companies and governments in the supplier countries and governments in the recipient countries. Arms sales are shrouded in secrecy. Apart from the occasional deal which might hit the headlines, most of us hear very little about the arms trade, still less about the effects of this trade.

The international arms trade falls into five categories:

- major arms (ships, aircraft, missiles, tanks).
- small arms (guns, ammunition, grenades etc.).
- 'dual use' equipment which may have a civilian as well as a military application, such as electronic communications equipment, computers and transport vehicles.
- spare parts, weapon training and maintenance.
- technology, chemicals and other raw materials and components used to manufacture weapons.[4]

The losers in the arms trade game

As mentioned above, the Third World provides arms traders with their main market. Some two thirds of the arms legally transferred around the globe are sold to Third World states (of which between a third and a half are destined for the conflict-ridden Middle East)[5]. For most people in the 'recipient' countries, this vast flow of arms has brought only misery. Largely ignored by the buyers and sellers, it is these human implications which form the focus of our study.

To what extent does the arms trade contribute to the high frequency of conflict in the Third World or to the poverty and repression haunting the lives of so many societies? And is there any prospect for future limitation of the arms trade to the Third World? These are some of the questions we have tried to answer in the chapters that follow, with particular reference to the British arms trade. Not only is Britain one of the world's leading arms traders but, more importantly, the bulk of its arms exports – 70 to 80% –[6] are sold to Third World countries.[7]

The leading exporters of major weapons to the Third World 1983–87. Countries are ranked according to 1987 exports. Figures are in US$million, at constant (1985) prices.

Source: *SIPRI Yearbook 1988* (Oxford University Press 1988)

	1983	1984	1985	1986	1987	1983–87
To the Third World						
1. USSR	6 889	7 310	7 754	8 065	9 697	39 714
2. USA	6 256	4 983	4 113	4 891	5 829	26 073
3. France	2 843	3 603	3 784	3 669	3 213	17 112
4. UK	579	1 139	942	1 263	1 641	5 564
5. China	961	1 180	872	1 302	1 040	5 356
6. FR Germany	1 175	1 835	520	613	630	4 773
7. Netherlands	—	57	38	132	495	722
8. Brazil	298	271	191	189	368	1 317
9. Sweden	20	49	39	145	302	555
10. Italy	970	811	539	325	228	2 873
11. Israel	384	252	152	179	201	1 168
12. Spain	545	400	119	202	177	1 442
13. Egypt	325	141	113	126	158	862
14. Czechoslovakia	99	122	37	89	133	481
15. Singapore	1	48	44	92	125	311
Others	1 293	756	511	405	487	3 452
Total	**22 638**	**22 957**	**19 768**	**21 687**	**24 724**	**111 775**

The leading Third World importers of major weapons 1983–87. Countries are ranked according to 1987 imports. Figures are in US$million, at constant (1985) prices.

Source: *SIPRI Yearbook 1988*

	1983	1984	1985	1986	1987	1983–87
Third World						
1. India	1 757	999	1 892	2 695	5 246	12 589
2. Iraq	3 003	4 157	2 935	2 100	3 541	15 736
3. Egypt	2 393	2 257	1 307	1 776	2 231	9 964
4. Saudi Arabia	1 121	970	1 526	2 495	1 753	7 865
5. Israel	357	290	192	406	1 632	2 877
6. Syria	1 868	1 598	1 634	1 782	1 301	8 183
7. Angola	443	568	444	720	1 126	3 300
8. Taiwan	592	378	574	664	607	2 815
9. South Korea	280	244	382	288	556	1 750
10. Peru	99	329	375	222	544	1 568
11. Thailand	360	309	310	91	520	1 590
12. Iran	347	277	535	618	519	2 297
13. Afghanistan	136	215	83	373	449	1 255
14. Brazil	24	22	21	293	428	788
15. Pakistan	321	656	675	864	424	2 940
Others	9 537	9 688	6 883	6 300	3 847	36 257
Total	**22 638**	**22 957**	**19 768**	**21 687**	**24 724**	**111 773**

Percentage şhares of the trade in major weapons with the Third World, 1982–86.

Source: *SIPRI Yearbook 1987* (Oxford University Press 1987)

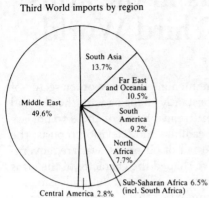

Third World imports by region

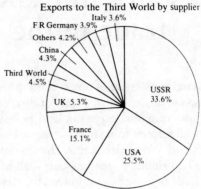

Exports to the Third World by supplier

NOTES

1: For the purposes of this study, Northern Ireland is included in the term, 'Britain' since arms companies in the six counties are subject to the same export controls as those in Britain and their exports are included in British government figures on the arms trade.
2: For convenience of generalisation, the 'Third World' is used to include all the countries in Africa, Asia (but not Japan or China), Latin America (including the Caribbean), and the Middle East (including Israel). Although Turkey's relationship to the arms trade is similar to that of other Third World states, this state is excluded from most of our Third World statistics which are mainly taken from Stockholm International Peace Research Institute (SIPRI) sources. SIPRI includes Turkey in the figures for European countries rather than the Middle East because of its NATO membership.
3: Legal = with government approval.
4: Nuclear weapons have been excluded from our study since there is, as yet, no significant nuclear arms trade. Similarly, the export of chemicals for the manufacture of chemical weapons will only be mentioned in passing. Our material focuses on the British arms trade and very little evidence exists, to date, of British involvement in the export of such chemicals or related technology.
5: Statistics on the arms trade are notoriously controversial. International comparisons, already difficult because of fluctuating currency exchange rates, differences in definition, and varying systems of national accounts, are further hampered by the secrecy which surrounds the trade. For example: the US Arms Control and Disarmament Agency figures in 1978 give developing countries' share of world arms imports at roughly three quarters of the total whereas SIPRI quotes the Third World share at two-thirds.
6: This is only an estimate based on figures included in The Defence White Paper 1988 on the value of British arms exports to different continents.
7: The effects of the arms trade on Britain, while also cause for concern, are *not* analysed in this study, nor are the motivations of supplier countries like Britain discussed in any great detail. These issues are covered in other CAAT publications.

CHAPTER 1

Current trends in the arms trade to the Third World

The arms trade is not a static phenomenon. Like any other sector of world trade, it is in a state of flux, constantly changing with the ebb and flow of global economic and political trends. Some of these trends are well known to us from newspaper headlines and television reports: the Third World debt crisis, the rise and fall of oil prices, warfare, government military spending cuts – all have shaped the character of the arms trade in recent years. Indeed the devastating effects of this trade can only be properly understood within the context of these global trends, some of which are analysed below.

Phase one – a superpower game

Since 1945 the arms trade has passed through three distinct phases. The first phase (1945 to 1973) was dominated by the two emerging superpower suppliers, the Soviet Union and the United States. It coincided with the intense superpower competition for global supremacy during the Cold War and the power vacuum left by decolonisation and the creation of new states. These factors combined to make arms transfers a potent tool for making new allies in the Third World and keeping 'friendly' governments in power. They were a key instrument of political influence in a period when direct rule was no longer acceptable. In this first phase, weapons were often given away, either as 'military aid' or under soft loan arrangements.

Phase two – oil means big business

The second phase in the arms trade (1973 to 1982) was one of rapid growth, largely because of the oil price rises in 1973 and 1979. This boosted revenues for Third World oil-producing governments (mainly in the Middle East). It also greatly increased the cash in the pockets of *non*-oil-producing Third World governments, as western banks, awash with 'petro-dollars' pouring in from oil-rich governments, made huge loans to the world's poorest states. A large proportion of the oil revenue accumulated by Middle Eastern governments and much of the credit doled out to Third World countries (around 20% according to SIPRI 1985) was used to buy arms.[1].

Until the early seventies, the Superpowers had believed that the strategic benefits of arming friendly nations overrode any financial loss incurred by giving weapons away. However, while both the United States and the Soviet Union continued to grant military aid, they now also started *selling* their military wares to those who could afford them. For the United States, many of the major customers of US arms were now wealthy oil-producing states to whom the US was no longer willing to supply arms as low-cost loans or grants. As an oil importer, the US was facing financial difficulties as a result of the oil price rise. Selling arms could thus help to mitigate such difficulties. Meanwhile the Soviet Union also started charging its richer oil-producing allies such as Libya in order to generate hard currency (ie. dollars) with which to purchase badly-needed Western technology. By the mid-1970s it had become standard practice to charge the full price for weapons, regardless of governments' revenues.

Countries in the Middle East have used petro-dollars to buy weapons

Rise of the British arms trade

The resulting shift from grants and loans to cash sales signalled the rise of the lesser arms suppliers such as Britain and France. For these countries, global strategic considerations, though still important, were no longer paramount and had been overtaken by commercial interests. As a result, their involvement in the arms export business only really gathered pace in this second phase when it became acceptable to *sell* weapons. The entry of the lesser suppliers into the arms trade eroded the superpowers' traditional markets, as Third World customers sought to diversify their source of arms. By buying from other suppliers, they could reduce the political restrictions or costs that came with purchasing weapons from either superpower. Although the United States and the Soviet Union continued to dominate the arms trade to the Third World, their share of the market in the seventies receded to around 70% and is now nearer 60%.[2]

Growth in 'high-tech' trade

Another striking feature of the arms trade in the 1970s was not just the quantity of arms exported, but also their *quality*. With more cash around, Third World countries could afford to splash out on more sophisticated weaponry. The drift towards arming Third World countries with the latest military models was set in motion in 1972 when the United States agreed to sell super-sophisticated Tomcat fighter aircraft to Iran. The next few years saw the sale of equally advanced American, Soviet and French top-of-the-line military equipment to other Middle Eastern countries. As a result of such sales, arsenals in a number of Middle Eastern states now resemble those of NATO or Warsaw Pact countries. Washington sold AWACS early warning radar aircraft to Saudi Arabia, for example, before it sold them to NATO.

But the richer Middle Eastern countries were not the only ones to stock up with high-tech weaponry in the 1970s. Looking at the SIPRI data on African arsenals in the 1960s, one finds that only two countries – Egypt and South Africa – were in possession of advanced aircraft and missile systems. Yet by the beginning of the 1980s, practically *every* African country had purchased at least one type of advanced weapon: more than a third could boast new or nearly new fighter aircraft and two thirds were equipped with some sort of missile system.[3] The transfer of sophisticated and highly expensive weaponry to the Third World has heightened tensions, particularly in the Middle East, and has placed a severe strain on Third World economies.

Phase three – Trading in a world recession

During the third phase of the arms trade (1980 to today), the demand for the most advanced weapons has remained high amongst Middle Eastern countries where regional arms races, conflict, and superpower rivalry have served to keep business brisk. Britain, for example, concluded huge deals with Jordan and Saudi Arabia in 1988 for advanced Tornado fighter aircraft. Nevertheless, it appears that the same rate of sales of major sophisticated weapons to the Third World has not been sustained outside the Middle East. In fact, since 1982, the total volume of major government-to-government arms transfers has declined. Excluding the five leading Third World importers – Iraq, Egypt, India, Syria, and Saudi Arabia (accounting for a combined 47% of Third World arms imports during 1982–86) – arms transfers to other Third World countries have dropped by over 25% in value.[4] This is mainly the result of a world economic recession which has hit Third World countries particularly hard. Government revenues throughout the Third World have plummeted under the crippling burden of interest payments on loans taken out in the 1970s. On top of the debt crisis, income for oil-producing countries has been slashed by an oil price drop in the mid-1980s. There has also been a steady depreciation in the international market value of many other raw materials (eg. coffee, copper, cotton) on which most Third World countries are dependent for export earnings. Quite simply, most Third World governments can no longer afford to buy major weapon systems.

Another factor behind the decrease in the sale of major weapons to the Third World is the *saturation* of Third World arsenals. The acquisition of advanced weaponry in the period 1972–82 has involved extensive training in the use, maintenance and repair of such weapons systems. This process, which normally takes several years, has effectively put a brake (albeit temporary) on the demand for new weapons systems.

Decline – what decline?

Yet the argument that the arms trade to the Third World is now in decline must be treated with caution. Instead of buying new weapons systems, many cost-conscious governments are choosing to re-fit and update existing stocks of weaponry. This is reflected in the large number of enhanced components and upgrading/modernisation kits now on the

Third World countries started to buy advanced weaponry in the seventies

Contra fighters on Nicaraguan border. High-tech weapons are not always appropriate in this terrain. *(Mike Goldwater/Network)*

market. Moreover, with the increasing transfer of military technology (rather than ready-made weapons) many Third World countries are now producing their own arms, and in so doing, are gradually cutting back on arms imports.[5]

Another trend which does *not* show up in the available data is the growing emphasis that Third World customers now place on the acquisition of less advanced equipment such as: helicopters, counter-insurgency planes, mobile missile launchers, small arms (machine-guns, rifles, etc.), ammunition and basic radio equipment. The reasons behind this change are easy to discern. Firstly, more basic weaponry is much cheaper and is therefore more attractive to debt-ridden governments. It is also less complicated to operate and repair, thereby saving time and investment in personnel training. The move back to low-tech equipment also reflects the unsuitability of much of the sophisticated weaponry on the market to the harsh climate and remote and rugged geography of many Third World countries. This is a key issue as the incidence of internal low-intensity or counter-insurgency warfare against guerilla armies grows. Counter-insurgency warfare is normally waged against small groups of guerilla fighters which, though ill-equipped, often operate in impenetrable terrain – mountains or deep jungle – where weapons such as tanks, supersonic jets and elaborate missile launchers are ineffective. On top of this, many armed forces involved in recent conflict have discovered that high-tech weapons do not function very well in wartime and are more prone to technological faults. During the Falklands War, for example, many of the modern missiles on both the British and Argentinian sides refused to work; Argentinian forces had to resort to dropping old-fashioned bombs. To use sophisticated weaponry, one also needs a high level of expertise and central command, neither of which can easily be maintained in the atmosphere of political chaos surrounding many wars.

Exports of ordinary infantry weapons are less likely to cause public concern than sales of supersonic jets and the like. But what is most striking about the weapons now being acquired by Third World countries is their utility for actual day-to-day combat operations – that is, for war fighting, rather than for deterrence or military modernisation. This build-up of basic war-making material will increase the risk that regional disputes will erupt in armed violence.

More and more traders

Another worrying aspect of the arms trade in the eighties is the sheer number of suppliers involved. The top four European exporters (France, Britain, West Germany and Italy) have been joined by a growing array of second-tier European suppliers. Spain, for example, now does a swift trade to the Third World with its sales of military trucks, armoured cars and transport aircraft. Neutral nations such as Sweden and Switzerland have also entered the market. Meanwhile, there are an increasing number of suppliers amongst the more industrialised Third World nations. Israel, Brazil, Egypt, Jordan, Libya, South Korea, North Korea, Syria, Singapore, and Indonesia are the main exporters.[6] These countries have steadily increased their share in total exports of major weapons to the Third World from 3.3% in 1977–81 to 4.5% in 1982–86. While the global economic recession continues, Third World suppliers are unlikely to increase their slice of the market much further since ultimately they cannot compete with the technology of the more industrialised countries, or with the generous credit terms offered by these countries. But by swelling the ranks of the arms traders, Third World suppliers have heightened competition in an already over-pressurised and shrinking market.

Trade out of control

'If the 1970s witnessed the explosion of the arms trade, the 1980s has witnessed its commercialisation,' writes researcher Raul Madrid[7], a phenomenon he attributes to the high number of sellers and the falling number of willing buyers for major weapon systems. In this cut-throat climate, arms companies, often aided and abetted by their governments,

Many governments have relaxed controls on the arms trade.

are hawking their wares with alarming aggressiveness and abandon.

Despite unwilling and often restrictive official attitudes towards the Third World arms trade, the western industrialised countries have found arms sales to developing countries too profitable to be shunned. In Britain and the US, the pressure to sell arms abroad was accentuated by cut-backs in orders from domestic armed forces as the military spending booms of President Reagan and Mrs Thatcher drew to a close. The same is true of other western European countries. In Sweden, for example, the Government has announced that the Swedish arms trade may be stopped altogether on moral grounds. Yet the same government allowed Swedish arms exports to double in 1987, with 34% of these exports sold to India, a country involved in a dangerous arms race with neighbouring Pakistan. Meanwhile, other western European countries have relaxed or lifted bans on controversial sales. Human rights violations are increasingly ignored in the name of business and countries embroiled in wars have been treated almost like any other customer. 'Who else is going to buy Spanish products like ammunition and fuses other than precisely those countries at war?' a Spanish arms trader' recently commented.[8] France, which imposed arms embargoes on the participants in the 1967 Arab-Israeli war and the Indo-Pakistani conflict, has shown little restraint in the Iran-Iraq war.

British arms export policy has also become more permissive, particularly since Margaret Thatcher came to power. An embargo against the sale of weapons to the brutal Pinochet regime in Chile was lifted in 1980, while in the case of the Gulf War, only the sale of 'lethal equipment' which could 'prolong or exacerbate the confict' was banned. This limited action did not prevent Government approval of export licences for a whole range of military equipment, including a sophisticated air defence radar system exported to Iran.

It appears that even the major world powers have now thrown political considerations to the wind, as the pressure to sell cuts across their traditional power blocs. Western European NATO members now export to Soviet allies such as Iraq, Libya and Mozambique, while the USSR is selling to traditionally western-aligned governments such as Jordan, North Yemen and Peru. These arms transfers are in most cases strictly commercial, involving no shift in alliances. As a result, the arms trade cannot so easily be manipulated as a political tool. Even some of the Superpowers' closest Third World allies are now rebuffing strategic control: Saudi Arabia and some other Gulf states have voiced opposition to US requests for bases, while Libya has appeared luke-warm to Soviet strategic proposals. When developing nations can easily shop for weapons elsewhere, they are reluctant to provide privileges to the superpowers and their allies. Meanwhile the major Third World exporters have outmanoeuvred even their counterparts in the industrialised nations by selling to almost any nation, placing next to no restrictions on their sales and frequently outbidding the other suppliers. Indeed, their relative success in recent years has *depended* on selling arms to countries which are normally shunned by other industrialised countries, such as Taiwan, Iraq and Iran. Brazilian arms companies have even used the lack of Brazilian Government control over the arms trade as a selling point. 'Brazil sells without any strings attached,' declares the president of Engessa, Brazil's largest arms company. 'We are not interested in a country's internal affairs or the human rights situation. We just go to sell.'[9] This pragmatic approach holds dangerous implications for international control of the arms trade. Arms embargoes against human rights violators such as South Africa or restrictions on sales to Iran and Iraq may still exert political pressure but have less practical effect than they used to because of the number of willing suppliers and governments now prepared to break such embargoes. One of the reasons why the Iran-Iraq war lasted so long is that the second-tier suppliers – Argentina, Brazil, Israel, China, North Korea and South Africa – were more than willing to refuel the belligerents, rapidly taking the place of the traditional suppliers (USSR, the USA and France) in the final stages of the war. A similar situation occurred in Central America in the late seventies where Israeli military imports helped to keep repressive regimes in El Salvador, Nicaragua (before the Revolution of July 1979) and Guatemala in power after the US Carter Administration had restricted sales to the region on moral grounds.

The increasing number of Third World suppliers means that the global arms trade is becoming more and more difficult to control. Yet since the bulk of the arms trade and much of the military technology – on which Third World arms traders are still dependent – emanate from the rich industrialised countries of the North, it is with them that the ultimate responsibility for controlling the arms trade remains.

Illegal and dual use trades

Fierce competition has also spurred the expansion of the illegal arms trade. With prolonged conflicts in Central America, Lebanon, southern Africa and the Persian Gulf, the demand for illicit arms from those governments or armed groups who cannot acquire equipment through legitimate channels has never been so great. The illegalities do not just occur in the shady underworld of gunrunners and white-suited millionaires. The use of private arms dealers, obscure shipping lines, middlemen and false end-user certificates [10] to disguise real destinations, are phe-

Private arms dealer in Pakistan *(Denis Doran/Network)*

nomena which can be found throughout the market. In their desperation to maintain sales, arms traders are increasingly prepared to indulge in irregular activities, often with the tacit approval or active involvement of governments, as was demonstrated by the Irangate scandal of 1987. In fact the secrecy and lack of control which surround the *legal* arms trade make it very easy to bend the rules.

Coupled with the illegal arms trade is the increase in what is described as the 'dual use' trade. This covers the sale of equipment which has a civilian, as well as a military application, such as helicopters, communications systems and transport vehicles. Like the illicit deals, this trade is supplying countries such as South Africa or Iran and Iraq which are affected by international sales restrictions. But the difference with the dual use trade is that it passes through *legal* channels under the guise of fulfilling a civilian function. So far, the British Government has turned a blind eye on the 'dual use' trade: it authorised the sale to South Africa, for example, of a Plessey mobile radar system (described by *Jane's Defence Weekly* as a 'weapon system') in 1981 and of a Marconi surveillance radar system in 1983, despite an international arms embargo against South Africa. The excuse given was that this equipment had a 'genuine civil application.' Yet the Marconi equipment was later photographed in operation at a military base in the Eastern Transvaal.

Although the illegal and dual use trades do not match the value of the official arms trade, their impact on the political and military events of the Third World is very significant. Those who receive arms through such channels are often forces attempting to overthrow democratically-elected governments (as in the case of the Contra forces in Nicaragua and Unita in Angola) or they are governments involved in wars and/or human rights violations (such as Iran, Iraq and South Africa). The illegal and dual use arms trade therefore serves to sustain violence and wars in a number of the world's trouble spots.

A buyers' market – perks and discounts

The increasing lack of control in the international arms trade is also related to the fact that the arms trade has turned into a buyers' market, in which the sellers must bow down to customers' requests or lose deals. One manifestation of this is the more flexible attitude which sellers now adopt towards their customers' payment problems, in the light of the debt crisis and falling commodity prices. Customers who previously had to pay in cash can now get arms on long-term credit, at concessionary interest rates. In 1986, for example, the US agreed to defer interest payments on credit related to arms. The British Government has also

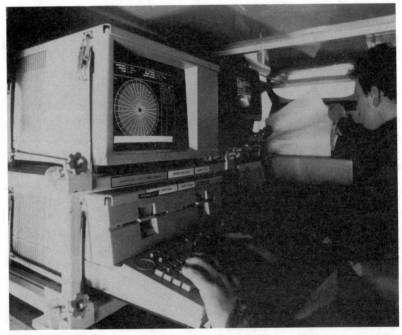

Military computer – an example of dual use equipment *(British Aerospace)*

extended its credit cover for major deals. In June 1988, an extra £1 billion of public money was made available to the British Government Export Credits Guarantee Department specifically 'to boost large overseas defence sales'.[11] The ECGD insures UK exporters against not being paid for weapons sold to overseas customers. It was only with heavy insurance cover from the ECGD that the recent £250 million deal concluded with Jordan for Tornado fighter jets could go ahead, as Jordan's external debt now stands at $3.8 billion.

In addition to favourable credit terms, recipient governments are also insisting that arms traders re-invest the money made on weapons sales in industrial projects in the customer country. This is a way of offsetting the heavy cost of purchasing sophisticated weaponry. In order to win a sale of 160 F-16 fighter aircraft to Turkey, the US company, General Dynamics, for example, had to invest in four Turkish hotels, a power plant and a fruit-exporting business. Britain's sales of £15 billion worth of Tornado aircraft to Saudi Arabia in 1985 and 1988 were conditional on British companies agreeing to invest around 25% of the value of the deals in Saudi industry. Such investment is of limited benefit to British trade: it is difficult to establish viable businesses in Saudi Arabia since most raw materials have to be imported and there is only a tiny market for finished goods owing to the region's small population.

Payment in kind, usually referred to as 'counter-trade' is another demand now being made by money-stretched customers. In Latin America, Israel has had to barter its weapons for Venezuelan oil and Argentinian beef. Likewise, Saudi Arabia only concluded the £10 billion Tornado deal with Britain in 1988 on the condition that Britain accept payment entirely in the form of oil. This proved of little benefit to Britain as oil was already very cheap at that time and Britain is still well-covered by North Sea oil for its fuel supplies.

As a further carrot to induce reluctant customers to buy their wares, arms traders are promising to help Third World customers establish their *own* arms industries. This development is explained in more detail in chapter 10.

Conclusion

In sum, today's arms trade is fast becoming a trade out of control. Third World customers' debt problems — often aggravated in the first place by expensive arms purchases — have caused the number of Third World government orders for major sophisticated weapons to decline from their peak in the early 1980s. This shrinkage in the volume of the arms trade has coincided with a surge in the number of arms suppliers, producing fierce and dangerous competition in an already saturated market. As a result, arms companies in the supplier countries, often in league with their goverments, are pushing sales to whoever they can in whatever way possible. Government controls on the legal arms trade are steadily being eroded while the use of illegal channels is becoming ever more prevalent. The consequence is that, despite the decrease in orders from some quarters, arms are being sold in *greater* quantities to governments who still have an insatiable appetite for weapons, such as those who are at war (until 1988 Iran and Iraq, for example) or those using military force to repress internal dissent. Meanwhile, other Third World governments who may be cutting back on sophisticated weapons are stocking up on low-tech weapons instead. It is small deals of low-tech weapons, more so than major ones, which provide the killing hardware of war. 'After all,' comments Aaron Karp of SIPRI. 'What is more deadly, one $25 million fighter aircraft or $25 million worth of rifles and ammunition?'[12]

NOTES

1: See chapter 5 on military debt.
2: *SIPRI Yearbook 1987*, Oxford University Press.
3: Robin Luckham: 'Rearmament and Militarisation in Africa' printed in *Africa Internacional: El Militarismo* Iepala 1986.
4: *SIPRI Yearbook 1987*.
5: See chapter 8 on Third World arms production.
6: See chapter 8.
7: Raul Madrid in *Multinational Monitor*, Feb. 1988.
8: Quoted in *El Pais* 31.3.88.
9: Jose Rivero quoted in *The Independent* 22.10.86.
10: End User Certificates are issued by the supplier government and specify who is buying the equipment, who will use it and what for. Often, the EUC is part and parcel of the signing of a deal. In Britain, it appears that the Government does not always insist upon an EUC being issued.
11: See *The Independent* 29.6.88.
12: *SIPRI Yearbook 1988*, p. 189.

CHAPTER 2

Why Third World countries buy arms

When analysing the arms trade to the Third World, there is one funda-mental question which precedes all others: *why* have Third World coun-tries felt a need to buy weapons in the first place? And why is it that the disastrous armament policies of the First World over the past century and the resulting bloodshed of two world wars have not discouraged the Third World from adopting the same militaristic policies? Part of the answer lies in some of the political upheavals that have taken place in the Third World since the Second World War.

Colonialism – legacy of militarism

The legacy of colonialism has been a prime ingredient in kindling a demand for weapons, particularly in Africa and Asia. During the pre-independence period, most colonies were disarmed by the imperial powers in order to prevent military uprisings from native populations. The Brussels Act of 1890 and the Saint Germain Convention of 1920, for example, forbade the supply of arms to anyone in Africa except to white settlers or colonial armies.

The absence of a national armoury stung the pride of new govern-ments in countries which became independent in the 1950s and 1960s. Many therefore strove to establish *indigenous* armed forces where none had existed previously. This policy immediately presented problems as none of the countries concerned had any industrial base for producing weapons locally. At that time, the *only* source of modern weapons was (and usually still is) the industrialised, former colonial powers of the North. Thus, when it came to equipping newly-formed armed forces in the Third World, the governments concerned imported the weapons from abroad. In SIPRI's view, the main reason for the 500% increase in major weapon imports to sub-Saharan Africa between 1950–54 and 1965–69 was 'the emergence of 27 new importing nations.'[1]

When looking more closely at Third World militarisation, one finds that the scars of colonialism run very deep. For example, the borders of countries in Africa, Asia, and the Middle East that became independent after 1945 were invariably based on artificial borders relating to the different colonial powers' spheres of influence and not to any natural

23

Military parade in Delhi. Arms are symbols of national pride. *(Sue Darlow/Format)*

geographical divisions between peoples and cultures. This meant that many newly independent states contained several different ethnic, racial and religious groups with which the newly independent government had to compete for its citizens' loyalties. Under such conditions, the armed forces and their imported weapons came to be regarded as the symbol of unity and national pride. In fact the utility of imported weapons as tools of destruction was often of secondary importance to the prestige which these weapons represented for new governments.

In many newly-independent states the educated, middle class elites who had acquired political power actually strove to model themselves on their former colonial masters, in military as much as in civil matters. This was to be expected as many of the leaders of these states had been trained in institutions like the British military college of Sandhurst. In newly-independent India, Mahatma Gandhi envisaged a very different role for the armed forces. In 1946 he wrote: 'Today they must plough the land, dig wells . . . (and do) construction work.'[2] However, the British-trained officer corps, organised on the patterns of their erstwhile colonial armed forces, refused to accept such a civic role. Since the primary function of the armed forces was to remain a military one, it was almost inevitable that they should be equipped with imported weapons.

Military rule

Most newly-independent governments started off on a very weak footing, rooted as they were in foreign, colonial systems rather than indigenous forms of government. Their fragility has since been accentuated by their subsequent failure to represent the interests of the majority of their populations. In the process of decolonisation, the imperial powers tended to transfer political and economic power to wealthy, western-educated and sympathetic elites. Scarce resources, already depleted by years of foreign exploitation, have since remained in the hands of these elites who have usually prioritised their own needs and not those of the general public. Faced with popular opposition, governments have frequently relied upon the armed forces to maintain themselves in power.[4] An obvious means of gaining or rewarding the support of the armed forces has been to purchase more weapons, thus swelling countries' arms imports and further strengthening the hand of the armed forces. In Egypt, for example, it has been claimed that the civilian government 'governs only with the backing of the armed forces.'[5] To keep the armed forces happy, its commanders are receiving a whole range of sophisticated weaponry.

In many countries, the armed forces have become so powerful that they have managed to seize power from civilian governments. In Africa, for example, by late 1984, 25 of the continent's 52 states were ruled either by military governments (22 states) or by governments of mixed military and civilian origin (3 states).[6] It is this military influence which partly explains the willingness of some countries to spend money on armaments rather than on economic development. The per capita mili-

Chilean military junta

tary expenditures of military-dominated governments are on average twice as high as those of other Third World countries.[7]

Perceptions of defence

'Third World states generally perceive themselves to be more vulnerable than their counterparts (in the industrialised world)' writes arms trade researcher, Chris Smith.[8] The reasons behind this sense of vulnerability are manifold. They range from internal tensions such as those between rich and poor or between different ethnic groups, to territorial disputes with surrounding countries (often aggravated by the artificial borders created by colonial powers) and perceived external political threats, such as a revolution or a military coup in a neighbouring country. Whatever the cause of the tension, the response is much the same as it has been in Europe at times of major political upheaval: rearmament. 'Third World states place great store on defence as a means of safeguarding political independence and territorial integrity'.[9] Arms imports are regarded as protection against a whole range of internal and external threats.

KENYA – A CASE-STUDY

Until the mid-1970s, Kenya's military spending was relatively low. However this all changed when Kenya felt itself to be under threat from neighbouring countries. Relations with Uganda deteriorated as that country, then under General Amin's rule, took a belligerent and aggressive stance towards Kenya. To the north, the revolution in Ethiopia was seen to be a threat to Kenya's western-biased social system, whilst to the south, relations with Tanzania became more difficult. Kenya's response was to re-arm. In 1976, President Kenyatta sent an urgent appeal to Britain for arms which resulted in the sale of £50 million of British military equipment to Kenya. Since then the Kenya armed forces have continued to expand with the help of British and US arms imports, including the training of Kenyan military personnel by UK armed forces.

Arms races

Importing arms to bolster security usually creates further *insecurity*, as neighbouring countries feel bound to buy yet more weapons to match the new arsenals on their borders. In Latin America, the re-emergence of a number of long-standing border disputes in the late sixties and seventies prompted many of the region's countries to purchase more weapons from abroad. However these arms purchases served simply to raise tensions even further and led to yet more arms purchases.[10] Similarly, in the Middle East, Syria and Israel remain locked in an arms race which continues to fuel more and more armament on both sides. In Syria, for example, as part of his drive to reach military parity with Israel, President Assad has spent 50% of his government's budget on imported arms. This all goes to show that a military build-up in one country and the regional arms race this provokes tends to act as a spur to further arms imports.

Secrecy

Another factor is the secrecy which surrounds the arms trade. Since there is no international register of arms transfers and very few reliable published details of individual countries' arms purchases, governments can never be sure what kind or quantity of arms its rivals may be purchasing. This causes suspicion and paranoia which often sets the tone for a regional arms race.

War boosts the arms trade

In any arms race there is always the danger that the build-up of arms will eventually provoke open warfare.[11] Once a war has broken out, the situation may then deteriorate into a vicious cycle with arms imports fuelling further conflict and conflict fuelling more arms imports. During a war, the belligerent forces are likely to purchase spare parts and new arms in greater quantities than in peacetime so as to replace weaponry destroyed in the fighting. Over three-quarters of the main importers of major weapons since the early 1970s have been involved in long-standing conflicts. Considering that the Third World has provided the battle-ground for nearly all the world's conflicts over the past forty years, the connection between war and the rise in Third World arms imports cannot be under-estimated.

Oil prices

Another boost to the Third World demand for weapons was the dramatic rise in oil prices during the 1970s. As their revenues rocketed, oil-producing governments – mainly in the Middle East Gulf region – wanted their armouries to reflect their newly-gained wealth and power. Foreign, and particularly US arms companies were only too pleased to oblige, faced as they were by a slump in sales at the end of the Vietnam war. By the end of the 1970s, such vast quantities of sophisticated weaponry had been sold to Iran, Iraq, Kuwait, Bahrain, Qatar, UAE, Oman and Saudi Arabia that these Gulf states alone accounted for half the Third World's military expenditure. But the effect of oil prices on arms imports has stretched far beyond the Gulf. Saudi Arabia, for example, has also used its petro-dollars to pay for the weapons ordered by other friendly governments, such as Jordan, Sudan, and Egypt (until 1979). Meanwhile, outside the Middle East, much of the oil money deposited by Gulf states in foreign banks was lent out to Third World governments who used these loans to buy weapons which hitherto had been beyond their reach.

Pressure from arms traders

Some have argued that western arms traders, in their eagerness to acquire the petro-dollars accumulating in the Middle East, themselves created a security-conscious climate so as to gain bigger arms sales.[12] Many of the big military spenders in the Gulf bought vast amounts of weaponry in the 1970s even though there was no immediate threat to their borders; most of the conflict at that time was taking place on the borders of Israel relatively far from the Gulf. This would suggest that Middle Eastern countries' 'defence requirements' have been partly created by arms companies and their political allies.

The extent to which Third World governments are pressurised by arms traders into buying weapons is difficult to assess. However it is clear that in the current atmosphere of recession and cut-throat competition, arms companies, with the active assistance of their governments, are pushing their wares harder than ever. 'The rise in Third World military spending has been urged on Third World Governments by a dangerous alliance of western governments and arms dealers', writes the peace researcher Ruth Sivard.[13] In most of the major arms-trading countries, special government departments have now been set up with the specific brief of promoting arms sales abroad.

British government promotion of arms sales

At a time when the global trade in major arms continues to shrink, many analysts have been puzzled by the relative success of the British arms trade in recent years. While other suppliers are struggling to remain buoyant, Britain's share of the market is steadily increasing and is expected to take a fifth of world business in 1988.[14] Huge billion pound deals were concluded in that year with Malaysia [15] and with Saudi Arabia, the latter worth £10 billion and representing Britain's biggest overseas order ever. How, then, should we account for Britain's record sales? According to Raymond Lygo, chief executive of British Aerospace,

it is partly to do with vigorous government promotion of the arms trade: 'What has helped enormously is that the Government, and particularly Mrs Thatcher, has worked endlessly to promote British industry.'[16]

British government promotion of the arms trade has been steadily increasing ever since the Defence Sales Organisation was established in 1966 within the Ministry of Defence to act solely as a sales promotion office for British arms. No other sector of British manufacturing industry receives such special treatment. Now called the Defence Export Services

British Army Equipment Exhibition.

Organisation and with a staff of 260 people, this department organises delegations of government ministers and civil servants to Third World countries, by way of promoting British arms sales in a more direct fashion. The DESO also gives advice to arms exporters on how to secure orders and gain government approval for an arms export licences. To give British arms companies an even bigger boost, it organises the biennial British Army Equipment and Royal Navy Equipment Exhibitions where potential overseas customers can survey British weapons.

On top of this, Britain also offers credit to potential buyers.[17] Without such credit facilities, it is hard to see how many of Britain's debt-ridden customers could afford British weapons.

Superpower motives

Supplier countries' strategic interests have also spurred the arms trade to the Third World. Nowadays, Britain and other western European countries are primarily involved in the arms trade for commercial reasons. The arms trade of the USA and the USSR, on the other hand, is motivated by strategic considerations almost as much as by economic gains. Since the fifties and sixties, arming the Third World has been regarded by the superpowers as a means of protecting economic, political and strategic interests in the Third World without direct rule. Thirty years ago, Third World governments were *dependent* on the superpowers and the former colonial powers for military supplies and were therefore particularly prone to political manipulation. As explained in chapter 1, the sheer number of arms suppliers in the eighties and fierce competition

MIDDLE EAST – STRATEGIC CROSSROADS

US and Soviet allies in the Middle East continue to receive vast amounts of weaponry in recognition of the region's strategic importance. Militarily, the Middle East is a potential security threat to the Soviet Union as the region borders on its territory. For the US, it is part of the 'forward defence line' against the Soviet Union and also represents the southern flank of NATO. On top of this, there is the Suez Canal, the shortcut between Europe and Asia, and the Middle East oilfields on which the industrialised world largely depends. This partly explains why Israel and Egypt are the world's largest recipients of US military aid and why Libya and Syria are the Soviet Union's biggest arms customers.

in the arms business have eroded the political influence of arms deals.

Nevertheless many US and Soviet arms transfers to the Third World are still motivated by superpower rivalry. US allies are persuaded to stock up with US weaponry and are then encouraged to use them to fend off the 'communist threat'; meanwhile Soviet allies are supposed to apply their military power to checking US influence. By tying the client to the supplying nation for training, spare parts, and maintenance of equipment, weapons can exert a surrogate political presence in Third World countries for many years after initial delivery. Hundreds or even thousands of technical and military advisors may accompany the weapon system. In Libya, for example, there are 8,000 Soviet military personnel and technicians keeping Libya's equipment in operation.[18]

Conclusion

Clearly there is no single reason why Third World governments import arms; their armament policies are determined by a number of different factors. Amongst these are: the colonial legacy, military rule, regional arms races, war, oil money, pressure from arms traders, and the political motives of the supplier countries. In greater or lesser degrees, all have played their part in the Third World arms bazaar.

NOTES

1: See SIPRI, *The Arms Trade with the Third World* (Almqvist and Wiksell: Stockholm 1971) p.50.
2: See SIPRI: *Arms production in the Third World* (Taylor and Francis, London 1986) p. 125.
3: See chapter 5.
4: See chapter 6.
5: Quote from Charles Richards in the *Financial Times*, 4.10.83.
6: See Ruth Sivard: *World Military and Social Expenditures 1987/88* (WMSE) (World Priorities, Washington 1987) p. 27.
7: See WMSE 1987/88 p. 26.
8: See Chris Smith: 'Third World arms control, military technology and alternative security' in SIPRI (ed. Thomas Ohlson): *Arms transfer limitations and Third World security* (Oxford University Press 1988).
9: See Chris Smith essay above.
10: See Nicole Ball: 'A Third World Responsibility' in *Arms Transfer limitations and Third World security*.
11: See chapter 9.
12: See Anthony Sampson: *The Arms Bazaar* (1977; reprinted by Coronet Books, UK 1988). Also, Altaf Gauhar: 'Weapons go where the money is' in *South* July 1982.
13: See WMSE 1985 p. 14.
14: Quoted in *The Sunday Times* 2.10.88.
15: The deal with Malaysia was for Tornado fighter aircraft and other equipment and was worth over £1 billion (See *CAAT Newsletter*, no. 93).
16: See *The Sunday Times* 2.10.88.
17: See chapter 1, p. 21.
18: According to *The Guardian* 8.5.84.

CHAPTER 3

Military Aid

Despite the explanations given in the previous chapter, it may still seem puzzling exactly how Third World countries, faced with spiralling debt, unstable commodity prices and even drought and famine, can continue to purchase weaponry from abroad. Loans and favourable credit facilities have been mentioned elsewhere in this book but there is another factor also worth considering: military aid. In 1985 43% of all aid was received by the Third World in the form of military-related assistance, most of which was granted by the US and the USSR.[1] It has already been stressed that the days when the superpowers gave most of their arms away are well and truly over: nowadays less than a quarter of weapons are traded on non-commercial terms. Nevertheless, military aid is still awarded to strategically important Third World allies, particularly where the super-powers wish to maintain a direct military presence. Invariably, military grants are used to secure access to ports and other facilities or to persuade the governments concerned to permit the location of military bases on their territory. Egypt's annual allocation of $1.3 billion of US military aid, for example, has been tied in with US plans to build a base for its Rapid Deployment Force in the Red Sea. Similarly the USSR has manipulated its generous donations of military equipment to South Yemen, Ethiopia and Angola with a view to gaining access to military facilities in these countries.

Military aid can take a variety of forms: direct aid; forgiven loans which never have to be repaid; or concessionary loans with very low interest rates and lengthy grace periods before payment begins.

British aid

Unlike the USA or the USSR, Britain is not in the habit of granting military aid, mainly because her commercial interests tend to override strategic considerations. Clearly it is more profitable to sell arms than to give them away. The Overseas Administration, through which the Government aid budget is channelled, insists that none of its money is available for military purposes and there is certainly no evidence of any Government aid being spent on an overtly military project. The only exception is a £9 million budget spent by the Foreign Office each year for the training and supervision of overseas military personnel. This enables training to be provided free of charge to countries of 'strategic importance', and, more significantly, to countries where there is a potential market for British military equipment.[2]

As the arms trade becomes more competitive, some British arms companies have called on the Government to use part of the aid budget to help their Third World customer governments pay for military contracts. They argue that this extra 'perk' would enable them to outbid foreign competitors. The pressure on the Government to change its policy is certainly mounting. According to *The Guardian*, Malaysia, which in 1988 concluded a £1 billion military deal with Britain, originally demanded that aid be included in the deal. Although the British Government turned down this request, an increase in UK aid to Malaysia through the Overseas Development Administration was the subject of parallel talks at the time that the military deal was announced.[3] It seems that the deal may have prompted these talks.

It could be argued that the groundwork for granting military aid has already been laid. At present, much of the aid budget is used to subsidise British companies trying to win orders in the Third World, with the result that 75% of our bilateral (government-to-government) aid is tied to buying goods and services from British companies. This means that funds provided by taxpayers for the world's poor are being used to bolster the British private sector and to finance lavish projects which are often inappropriate to the needs of local people. With a government

Hydro-electric dam in Brazil, catering for foreign companies. Bilateral aid does not always benefit local people.

which appears primarily concerned about the benefits of the aid budget to British companies, it may not be too long before arms contracts are also awarded subsidies. As we mentioned in chapter 1, the Government Export Credit Guarantee Department is already in the business of using taxpayers' money to underwrite British arms deals.

US aid

US military aid and subsidised loans under the Pentagon's Foreign Military Sales Programme more than doubled in the first Reagan term from $3.2 billion in 1981 to over $6.4 billion in 1984, boosted by the Administration's commitment to arm and train anti-communist governments and rebel movements. In 1981, US aid was split 50:50 between military aid and development assistance but under Reagan this proportion swung to 64:36 in favour of military aid.[4] Since then, huge debts and overspending in the US military sector have now forced the Administration to cut back its military aid budget. Nevertheless, grants to strategic allies and governments perceived to be under threat from left-wing forces remain high. During the fiscal year 1988–89, El Salvador, whose armed forces are renowned for repeated human rights abuses, received $270 million in US military aid compared to $110 million in economic aid.[5] 'While domestic (US) farmers or students from low income families have been finding it harder and harder to get government subsidised

US troops in Honduras *(Joe Fish)*

loans,' writes researcher William Hartung, 'dictators in search of the latest in US weapons technology have had a considerably easier time of it during the Reagan years.'[6]

ELVIA ALVARADO, HONDURAN PEASANT WOMAN:

'The millions of dollars the gringos (US Aministration) send don't help the poor campesinos. The money isn't used to create jobs so that everyone can work. Instead the money is for arms, for aeroplanes, for war tanks. But we don't eat aeroplanes, we don't eat tanks, we don't eat bullets. The only things we campesinos eat are corn and beans. So what good are all those weapons?'[7]

Soviet aid

Recently the USSR has been less willing to grant military aid to its allies as it is now increasingly dependent on the income generated from *sales* of arms. Yet an exception is made for a few favoured clients whose strategic or political importance overrides commercial considerations. India and South Yemen, for example, can purchase Soviet equipment under 'soft currency' credit terms which means that they are not obliged to pay in dollars. Repayment periods are also very long. Nicaragua appears to have received some of her Soviet equipment free of charge (as did Grenada before the US invasion in 1983) while Angola was granted a two-year moratorium in 1986 on its $2.1 billion military debt. In some cases, Soviet allies who have no means of paying for weapons can trade raw materials for arms under what are known as counter-trade agreements.[8] A British visitor to Mozambique in 1986 commented on the effects of one such Soviet counter-trade agreement: 'the principal Russian interest is hoovering fish out of Mozambiquan waters to the point where the people are seriously short. In return, the Soviet Union supplies arms. But one cannot eat arms.'[9] Meanwhile the USSR's military facilities in Vietnam are thought to be in part-payment for arms deliveries.

Conclusion

Despite the arms suppliers' preference for selling weapons, military aid in its varying forms clearly remains a convenient method of arming friendly states. The superpowers have granted military aid primarily for political reasons but it is conceivable that other arms-supplying governments in Europe, for example, will be tempted to grant military aid for commercial reasons. In the current climate of fierce competition and depressed sales, arms traders are likely to put pressure on their governments to dip into aid budgets so as to cushion the cost of weapons to customers with financial difficulties.

NOTES

1: See Ruth Sivard: *World Military and Social Expenditures 1986* (WMSE) (World Priorities, Washington 1986).
2: See chapter 7.
3: David Fairhall, Defence Correspondent, in *The Guardian*, 28.9.88.
4: See *New Statesman* 17.5.85.
5: Figures compiled by Jesuit University of Central America, San Salvador.
6: William Hartung in *Multinational Monitor*, February 1988.
7: Elvia Alvarado quoted in *Don't be afraid, Gringo – A Honduran woman speaks from the heart*. Translated and edited by Medea Benjamin, Food First Book (Institute for Food and Development Policy), San Fransisco 1987.
8: See chapter 1 under heading, 'A buyer's market'.
9: Letter to *The Guardian* 21.7.86.

CHAPTER 4

Arms can kill without a shot being fired – effects on development

'You gringos are always worried about the violence done with machine guns and machetes. But there is another kind of violence that you must be aware of too. To watch your children die of sickness and hunger while you can do nothing is a violence of the spirit.'

– A Salvadorean peasant in conversation with US pacifist Charles Clements

Third World military spending boom

Hand in hand with the expansion of the global arms trade over the past forty years has come the massive rise in Third World military spending. In 1965, the proportion of global arms spending accounted for by Third World countries was 6%. By 1982 it had crept up to 20%, falling only slightly to 18% in the mid-1980s.[1]

The expense of major weapons

The arms trade provides a key to the swift rate at which Third World arms spending has risen. It is no accident that the tripling of the Third World spending figure between 1965 and 1982 coincided with a boom in the arms trade.

By definition, major weapons nearly always cost a lot of money. Since they are sold almost exclusively to governments, they are shielded from the competitive pricing of the consumer goods market and are rarely subject to adequate government price controls. This was illustrated by the infamous story uncovered by a US Congressman in 1985 of the $659 ash trays, $640 toilet seat, and the $7,400 coffee pot supplied by

Communal tap in a shanty town, Chile. Military spending can reduce social spending.
(Chile Solidarity Campaign).

Grumman Aerospace to a US naval air station.[2] It is therefore not surprising that a large slice of Third World military spending has been taken up by arms purchases.

Out of the $160 billion spent on military purposes by Third World countries in 1985[3], $30 billion was used to pay for arms imports[4] which is more than the total sum received by the Third World in economic aid.[5] On top of this initial expenditure, there was considerable spending on the infrastructure needed to support these weapons: roads, docks, harbours, airfields, hangars, and training programmes for military personnel in the operation and maintenance of the weapons. The real amount of money spent on arms imports by Third World countries is thus far above the initial $30 billion doled out for the weapons themselves.

The military – a top priority

Mounting debts and shrinking revenues have now started to trim down the Third World proportion of global military spending. However the decrease since 1982 is deceptive: military expenditure is still alarmingly high in relation to other expenditures on health, education, housing and agriculture. In many cases, the *proportion* of government revenue devoted to military purposes is *rising*, as other public expenditures are reduced in order to maintain the military budget. In 1972, those countries with the lowest per capita national income spent 17.2% of their state budget on military purposes as compared with 12.7% for education and 4.6% for health care. In 1983 the corresponding figures had tilted even further in favour of the military and read 19.5% (military), 4.7% (education) and 2.7% (health).[6] This suggests that in times of economic recession, priority is given to the military complex by diverting resources away from precisely those state services which have catered for the poorest sectors of Third World societies.[7] Worsening poverty is the inevitable outcome of this policy.

Effects of military spending

Heavy military spending is a drain on any economy but its effects are particularly acute in Third World countries where meagre state budgets and infrastructures are already stretched. Many people forget that military outlays fall into the category not of investment but of *consumption*, since they produce nothing which can be exchanged for other goods or services. Weapons can only be used for destruction; if not engaged in warfare, they merely languish in armouries, performing no active role in the economy whatsoever. This means that military spending is dead-end expenditure which serves merely to deprive productive sectors of the economy such as agriculture or civil industry of investment.

Military spending also fuels inflation since it generates income (ie. cash) for those companies and individuals working in the military complex but no goods or services on which the income can be spent. Inflation is caused by too much money chasing too few goods.

Imported arms distorting development

Weapons purchases encourage the expansion of a military complex which may be of little relevance to the largely rural civilian population. For example, if a government spends millions of dollars on new tanks, it makes sense to build roads so that the tanks can be transported to the country's borders or to other obvious points of attack. Such roads will link strategic points like cities, ports and border points and may improve

EXAMPLES

Nearly 50% of the world's arms exports end up in the Middle East where the economic and social effects of heavy military spending are starting to bite. In **Egypt** and **Libya** a drop in world oil prices has slashed those governments' revenues and triggered their worst economic crisis in years. Egypt's debt now stands at $40 billion, a quarter of which is owed on military imports. In 1987, under pressure from the International Monetary Fund, the Egyptian government was considering the removal of $7 billion worth of food subsidies on which millions of Egyptian people are dependent. Yet there have been no cutbacks in the $5 billion military budget.

Meanwhile Libya's leader, Colonel Gadhafi, has responded to economic crisis by adopting vigorous austerity measures on the domestic front, leading to rising food prices and shortages in the shops. In 1985 it was announced that dozens of civilian contracts for projects like roads and railways were to be cancelled. Yet despite the economic squeeze, the military budget still accounts for about half the overall government budget.

Syria is also suffering under the burden of a military budget which consumes 50% of the total government budget. In the cities there are shortages of basic commodities such as sugar and rice and many factories have closed for lack of raw materials. Five-hour power cuts are scheduled each day and water is cut off at night. Syrians living abroad are being encouraged to send medicinal drugs home. A journalist recently described the Syrian economy as a hostage to President Assad's determination to reach military parity with Israel.[8]

the country's long-distance communications but may bear no relation to the needs of rural people, many of whom still live in isolated villages with no proper access even to the nearest market town. Sometimes communities are actually uprooted in order to make way for such roads. The construction of military roads, like the building of military airports, harbours and hangars, frequently takes priority over the building of schools, hospitals and socially useful projects in countries with only limited building materials and skilled construction workers.

THIRD WORLD MILITARY SPENDING –
FACTS AND FIGURES

In 1985, a study of 141 countries revealed that those with the highest percentage of military spending in relation to their Gross National Products (GNP) also have the highest infant mortality rates.[9]

United Nations researchers have estimated that in a country with a population of 8.5 million and an annual per capita income of $350, because of the diversion of resources which arms imports represent, every $200 million of arms imports are indirectly responsible for about 20 still-births per 1,000 births, 14 illiterates per 1,000 adults and a reduction of the average life-span by 3–4 years.[10]

Economist Saadet Deger claims that Mexico, with a lower per capita income and a very low military burden, compares favourably in nearly all quality of life indicators with its Latin neighbours, Brazil and Argentina, which have higher per capita national income, as well as higher military burdens. Tanzania which has a relatively low military burden and only a quarter the per capita national income of oil-rich Nigeria manages to outstrip Nigeria in nearly every quality of life comparison.[11]

ELVIA ALVARADO, HONDURAN PEASANT WOMAN:

'A lot of money the U.S. sends (Honduras) is used to build roads. But they're mainly interested in building roads that lead to the military bases or the Nicaraguan border (war-zone) . . . Why don't they build roads in other parts of the country, like in the villages where the poor campesinos (peasants) live? When you want to get to a campesino village, you might have to walk three or four hours straight uphill on dirt tracks. If a road isn't important for the government or the Gringos (US armed forces), forget it. It never gets paved.'[12]

Drought in India. Many governments import more arms than agricultural equipment.
(TUIREG)

Wasted skills

One of the most serious implications of importing arms is the resulting drain on the skilled workforce. A large proportion of the technical workers in Third World countries are fully occupied in operating or maintaining imported weapons. In the Gulf Co-operation Council states,[13] where arsenals are bulging with high-tech weapons, more people work for the military than in any other sector except farming, with 30% of Saudi men employed in military-related jobs.[14]

Rural drain

In the same way that resources flow from less developed countries to the industralised ones, arms imports drain Third World *rural* areas of income for the benefit of Third World *cities*. This is very serious as the income of most non-industrialised Third World countries largely depends on the export of raw materials or cash crops (eg. cotton, coffee, tobacco, bananas, rice) produced in rural areas.

Third World governments usually pay farmers in local currency for the cash crops they produce. Yet the foreign exchange (ie. dollars worth more than the local currency) which the Government then generates by exporting these crops is not always reinvested in agriculture. Instead it is often used to buy arms from abroad. The only people to profit from

Women suffer most from high military spending. *(Christian Aid)*

these arms imports are those belonging to a small city-based elite (military bureaucrats in the government and armed forces, technical workers involved in the maintenance of the weapons and persons engaged in local military industry) while virtually no benefits are returned to the countryside. According to the United Nations, many developing countries use five times as much foreign exchange for importing arms as they do for importing agricultural equipment.[15] This gives us some idea of the huge loss of productive investment posed by arms imports to economies whose wealth still rests on agriculture.

A man's world

Most governments, armies and military companies are predominantly male institutions. This means that women have very little control over government military budgets. With limited access to the echelons of power, they have great difficulty in preventing the diversion of resources away from social services which high military spending provokes. Yet it is women who bear the brunt of inadequate health facilities, education, housing and water supplies.

Heavy military spending also affects women's employment prospects. State service sectors such as health and education are often major targets for the public spending cuts effected to protect the military budget. One of the commonest ways of curbing spending in these sectors is to reduce the number of workers. Significantly, it is precisely in these state service sectors where women often form the bulk of the workforce. Most nurses and teachers, for example, are women. Outside the service sector, women tend to occupy the least secure jobs, often working on a part-time or seasonal basis in the most exploitative conditions. When heavy military spending aggravates a general economic crisis, their jobs are the first to go. The repercussions on the family unit are crippling as most women enter the workforce out of economic necessity and many are the sole supporters of their children.

Conclusion

The arms trade to the Third World harms millions of people, even if the weapons exported are never used. Because of their expense, arms imports monopolise government funds, already paltry in most Third World countries. Less money is then allocated to those items of public spending intended to meet people's basic needs such as health and education. As the arms trade has expanded, more and more wealth, resources, skills and jobs have been concentrated in the servicing of weapons rather than people.

NOTES

1: John Turner and SIPRI: *Arms in the '80s* (Taylor and Francis, London 1985) p. 11.

2: See *Financial Times*, 30.5.85.

3: Ruth Sivard, *World Military and Social Expenditures 1987–88* (WMSE) (World Priorities, Washington 1987) p. 42.

4: Richard Grimmett, 'Trends in Conventional arms transfers to the Third world by major supplier, 1978–85' (Congressional Research Service, Washington, 9.5.86) p. 31.

5: Ruth Sivard: *WMSE 1986* (World Priorities, Washington 1986) p. 12.

6: World Bank: 'World Bank World Development Report 1986' (Washington 1986, p. 222).

7: The International Monetary Fund has encouraged this diversion of resources. See chapter 4 on Arms and Debt.

8: Judith Vidal-Hall in *South*, July 1988.

9: *The Lancet* 15.6.85.

10: Quoted in Hungarian Peace Council Report: 'Disarmament through Development Forum 1987'.

11: Saadet Deger and Somneth Sen: 'Defence, entitlement and development' in *Defence, Security and Development* – ed. S. Deger and R. West (Frances Pinter, London 1987).

12: Elvia Alvarado quoted in *Don't be afraid, Gringo – A Honduran woman speaks from the heart*. Translated and edited by Medea Benjamin (Food First Books, 1987).

13: Gulf Co-operation Council states: Bahrain, Kuwait, Oman, Qatar, Saudi Arabia, United Arab Emirates.

14: *Middle East Report* (MERIP), Jan./Feb. 1987.

15: See 'Disarmament' vol. IX no. 2.

CHAPTER 5
Military spending and debt

At the opening debate of the UN General Assembly in 1984, a number of Third World delegates warned that the debt problems of the developing world were as serious a threat to international instability as the arms race. 'A world in which politics is replaced by arsenals and economy by finance is simply a world in danger' stated President Alfonsin of Argentina.[1] But a world in even greater danger is one in which the build-up of arms is actually intermeshed with the debt crisis.

Background to the arms-debt link

It was the paralleled expansion of the arms trade and of indebtedness in Third World countries towards the end of the 1970s which gave rise to the suspicion that the arms sector was a major contributing factor to the debt crisis. The historical background to the global financial crisis may give us some clue to this connection.

It all started in the early 1970s when a sharp rise in oil prices vastly increased revenues for the world's oil producers. The governments concerned poured much of this money into the coffers of Western banks in order to accumulate interest on their petro-dollars. But banks can only generate interest for their customers by re-lending the money deposited with them. Thus, desperate to re-invest the petro-dollars, the western banks started to make huge loans to the world's poorest countries. They are now extracting vast sums from these countries in the form of interest payments on the loans.

Initially, Third World governments expected to repay the loans quite quickly by increasing their own exports, consisting mainly of raw materials. However, when recession hit the industrialised countries in the early 1980s, the demand for raw materials fell while at the same time interest rates soared, thereby crippling Third World economies. Payment of the interest on the loans – let alone repayment of the loans themselves – became a bitter struggle if not an impossibility for most Third World countries. By 1985, the World Bank calculated that their combined external debt had reached $1 trillion ($1,000,000,000,000).

Where did the loans go?

But the inability to repay debts is not just the result of a world recession or a rise in interest rates. It also bears some relation to what the loans were spent on in the first place. Some of the money was used to pay for essential imports like oil and some to finance so-called 'development' projects which were usually intended to boost cash-crop farming for export. But a significant proportion of the loans was also used to finance weapons purchases. In this they were greatly encouraged by the world's arms companies and the exporting countries' governments.[2] Between 1972 and 1982, precisely the period of increased Third World borrowing, the value of arms transferred to non-oil developing countries more than *doubled* in real terms.[3] Since arms can only be used for destruction, the arms imports of the 1970s have not generated any wealth and have therefore done nothing to repay debts. In fact, the purchase of expensive weapon systems has often led to *further* borrowing.[4]

Military debt figures

It is difficult to give a reliable figure for the military share of a country's debt, since the financial terms of arms deals are rarely revealed and the OECD (Organisation for Economic Co-operation and Development) and World Bank statistics do not usually include military debts. Moreover much of the military debt has been financed not through official military credits but through private credits arranged with banks and other commercial financial institutions. Nevertheless, it has been estimated that had they bought no arms during the period 1972–82, non-oil developing countries would have had to borrow 20% *less* each year.[5]

FACTS AND FIGURES

High military spenders such as Sudan, Mauritania, Peru, and Vietnam were among the first to default on their debt repayments.[6]

According to the United Nations, two-thirds of funds lent to Thailand in recent years have been devoted to military purposes.[7]

SIPRI reports that arms purchases have played a major role in the financial difficulties of Chile and Argentina.[8]

Military loans

In Egypt, 25% of the country's $40 billion debt is owed on military imports. This is because a large proportion of loans transferred to Egypt from Britain, France and the US, have only been offered on condition that the Egyptian Government spend the money on military equipment from the supplier arms factories. These military loans have proved very lucrative to western arms companies, who without such credit cover, would have been unable to do business with a debt-ridden country like Egypt. They have also favoured western banks: until recently on the annual $1.3 billion US military loan to Egypt, American banks were raking in $600 million in interest payments. This is almost as much as Egypt receives each year in economic aid. Because of this Middle Eastern country's strategic importance, the US has now written off the interest payments on its military loans to Egypt. But other indebted countries have not been so lucky and continue to pay dearly for their military loans.

As the volume of the global arms trade begins to shrink, arms-producing countries are more and more willing to offer military loans to Third World governments so as to enable their customers to buy arms. The involvement of the arms trade in the Third World debt crisis is therefore likely to increase.

IMF and World Bank policies

In view of the adverse effect of arms purchases on a country's ability to repay its debt, one would expect the world's financial institutions to discourage their debtors from setting such lavish military budgets. Yet matters concerning 'national security' appear to be sacrosanct. Turning to the International Monetary Fund for short-term loans to tide them over, Third World governments find that loan conditions include a removal of government food subsidies, cuts in health and education services and reductions in wages – all measures designed to extract more money from the poorest sectors of society. But a slimming military diet is rarely included in these conditions. Meanwhile, local populations are not paying in pounds or dollars, but through greater hunger, lower wages, less health care and declining education provision for their children.

US military debt

On the issue of military spending, the creditor countries are hardly in a position to set an example. Much of the enormous $2 trillion deficit accumulated by the USA, the world's biggest debtor, has arisen from its colossal military budget and from large-scale borrowing for the Star Wars programme. Since the Reagan administration refused to finance its military budget with additional taxes, it was only able to raise the required cash by persuading the rest of the world to invest in the US. To this end, the US has had to offer high interest rates which, in turn, have kept

interest rates high worldwide. The US military budget is therefore partly responsible for the huge amounts of interest Third World countries have had to pay on their loans and for the resulting hardship inflicted on Third World people.

Debt – an instrument of war

When the United States' own debt is almost twice that of all Third World countries, one may wonder why so much importance is attached to Third World debt and why the pressure on such countries to service their debts is so great. One explanation may be that the creditor countries see political advantages in maintaining the debt crisis, as debt expert, Susan George, has suggested.[9] She argues that although the Third World now collectively owes about a trillion dollars to the North, in today's world, this is *not* very much money. On Black Monday, Wall Street lost as much, on paper, in a single day.

Susan George believes that debt is used as a tool to weaken Third World countries. In her view, the so-called 'debt crisis' neatly fits Karl von Clausewitz' definition of war. Not only does it allow 'the continuation of politics by other means' but it also forces 'the adversary to do our will.' Above all it prevents serious challenges to the dominant world system. For example, when President Arias of Costa Rica announced his peace plan for Central America, the United States (which opposed the Peace Plan) immediately slapped unusually strict bans and restrictions on Costa Rican exports and refused, for the first time, to intervene with US commercial banks on Costa Rica's behalf. With $4.5 billion worth of debt to service – a huge sum of money for a small country – Costa Rica now finds itself ineligible for further bank loans. As a result, other indebted governments may well think twice before initiating political plans unwelcome to a major creditor like the United States.

Conclusion

A large proportion of the petro-dollars lent out to Third World governments in the seventies – 20% according to SIPRI estimates – was spent on arms. These purchases have generated no wealth with which to pay back loans, causing Third World countries to fall into even greater debt. The main international lending institutions, while imposing restrictions on their debtor governments' *civil* public spending, have made few attempts to reduce these governments' military spending budgets. Debt expert, Susan George, questions the underlying motives of the International Monetary Fund and its political backers: as far as she is concerned, debt is simply war by other means.

NOTES

1: Quoted in 'Military-Related Debt in Non-oil Developing Countries' by R. Tullberg in *Arms and Disarmament SIPRI findings* ed, Marek Thee (Oxford University Press, New York 1986).
2: See chapter 2.
3: 'Military-Related Debt in Non-oil Developing Countries' (see note 1).
4: See chapter 6.
5: R. Tullberg in *SIPRI Findings* (see note 1).
6: U.N. Development Forum 1984.
7: U.N. Development Forum November 1985.
8: R. Tullberg in *SIPRI Findings*.
9: Susan George in a paper given at a conference on US imperialism at Sheffield University, May 1988. See also her book, *A Fate Worse Than Debt* (Penguin, London 1988).

CHAPTER 6
Poverty – repression – militarisation

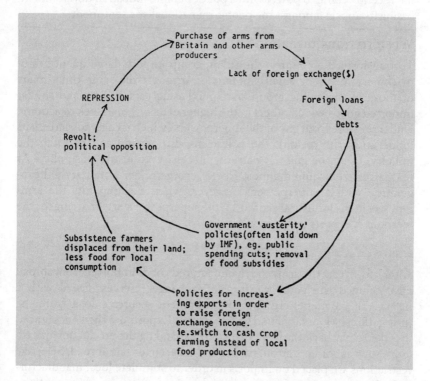

It could be argued that the pressures resulting from heavy military spending such as high inflation, rising debts and increased social inequality can only be dealt with by governments prepared to repress the discontent it brings about.[1] If so, it may be more than mere co-incidence that many big arms-importing governments are not only plagued by debt and balance of payment problems but are also responsible for repeated human rights violations.

To illustrate the connections between poverty, repression and arms imports, we shall refer to the history of an imaginary country whose experience bears close resemblance to that of many countries in the Third World today.

Post-colonial period

After World War II, country X builds up a small foreign exchange surplus, rudimentary armed forces and a police force. The country's economy is based on agriculture, predominantly small farms run by peasant families, but also including a few large, colonial-style estates primarily producing cash crops for export such as coffee and tobacco. A civilian political party has recently come to power with a policy of rapid industrial development, basing its appeal amongst the people on nationalistic sentiment.

Western transformation

To transform the country, the ruling group imports large quantities of machinery including small amounts of arms. At the same time, many of those in the ruling group start purchasing cars, radios, and similar imported goods which others in the higher echelons then seek to acquire. Under pressure from one of the superpowers (which is eager to increase its influence in the region), the politicians also expand and re-equip the military, using the guise of patriotic 'necessity' to justify this policy. At first, arms are acquired almost free of charge under a military aid programme with a superpower. However, when a slump hits the arms industry in the industrialised world, the superpower starts charging for the weapons it exports to country X.

Loans

After a few years the arms and manufactured goods imported from abroad have drained the country's foreign exchange reserves. Faced with a balance of payments crisis, the Government secures a loan from the International Monetary Fund to tide it over. Exports are then encouraged in order to pay back the loan, mainly by expanding the production of cash crops such as coffee, cotton, rubber and tobacco for sale abroad. Selective restrictions are placed on imports in order to stimulate local manufacturing industry, the sole exception of this being arms imports which continue to increase unchecked. Thriving on the prestige and military heavyweight of these arms imports, the influence of the army continues to grow.

IMF prescription

Despite a short-term improvement, a steady decline in the price of cash crop exports relative to manufactured imports, leads to yet another huge deficit. The problem is aggravated by a sharp rise in both the price of imported oil and the interest rates to be paid on the IMF loan. In desperation, the government turns to the IMF yet again for a further loan. This is granted on condition that import restrictions on foreign manufactured goods are removed for the benefit of western companies and state incentives provided for cash crop production (so as to boost export earnings). The Government is also ordered to reduce its public expenditure by cutting already meagre state assistance such as health services, education and food subsidies.

Repercussions

The results of these new policies are as follows:

Local Industry destroyed

The removal of import controls destroys the embryonic local industry as large foreign companies flood the markets with their glossy, western-style advertising.

Less food, less land

Several large tracts of land, most of which were previously farmed under the traditional system, are bought up by a few individuals and firms, eager to capitalise on the government's new incentives for cash crop farming. These rich farmers rapidly convert the land to the production of one single crop – either tobacco or coffee – for export. To make way for these commercial estates, thousands of families with smallholdings lose their land. Many have rented their plots from the big landowners for generations and now find they have no legal entitlement to ownership. Some are forcibly evicted while others are harrassed until they leave.

Most smallholding families used their land primarily to grow food – not just for their own consumption but also for local populations as they sold their surplus grain and vegetables in nearby markets. But now this system has broken down. Since one cannot eat coffee or tobacco (the region's cash crops), there are shortages of basic supplies, both in the town and the country. As a result, provisions have to be imported either from other regions of the country or from abroad. Even rural people now have to *buy* their food. They have no control over the prices which are determined either by the central government department responsible for food distribution or by big landowners with a monopoly over the market. Open to exploitation, thousands of families fall into debt and poverty.

Landless labourers

The families who were thrown off their land have now joined the pool of landless labourers drifting from one cash-crop estate to another in search of paid work. On the estates, wages are low and conditions often appalling. Workers are housed in prison-like barracks with no proper sanitation and

Tea-picking in Sri Lanka. Much of the agricultural land in the Third World is used for cash crops. *(Jenny Matthews/Format)*

are forced to purchase bad quality food and supplies from a plantation store where prices are high. Many families are constantly in debt to the store. Workers are hired and fired at the employers' whim and many can only find work in the peak harvest times. This means they have to migrate from one region to another, leading to the uprooting of entire communities and to the disintegration of the family unit.

A drift to the towns

A sudden drop in world coffee and tobacco prices then forces down wages on the estates even further. Unable to make ends meet, many farm labourers head for the city. Some find work in newly-established factories (many of them belonging to foreign multinational companies) but in the absence of any large-scale industry, thousands of rural immigrants fail to find work. Instead they scratch out a living on the margins of the economy, selling anything from sweets to biros in the street or doing odd jobs. In the shadow of westernised city centres, they set up house in makeshift hovels which constitute the sprawling shanty towns.

IMF policy bites

Conditions rapidly deteriorate for these rural immigrants. Under pressure from the IMF, the Government has cut state services. Requests for health services, electricity and running water for the shanty towns fall on deaf ears. Another facet of IMF policy is that those lucky enough to have found paid work now have their wages frozen, despite mounting inflation. The crunch comes when the Government decides to remove all subsidies on basic foods leading to sharp price rises.

Protest

Unrest breaks out in the poorer areas of the cities. On the whole this takes the form of peaceful protest such as demonstrations or strikes but the Government decides to crack down hard. The president declares an emergency and has the opposition suppressed: union leaders and political opponents are arrested and censorship is tightened.

Shanty town, Chile

PROTEST AGAINST DOMESTIC POLICIES

'Thousands of Guatemalans marched through the streets of the capital to protest against government measures which have pushed up the price of petrol and basic foods.'
– The Independent 6.7.88

'In Rio de Janeiro, there were more than 30 supermarkets, bakeries and chemist shops looted in one month alone in 1983.'
– International Labour Reports, Sept.–Oct. 1984

'In the Dominican Republic more than 50 people died in April 1984 when large-scale rioting broke out in protest against price rises. Following IMF policies, the government had doubled and tripled the prices of many essential items.'
– ILR Sept.–Oct. 1984

'Ecuadorean President Leon Febres Cordero on Tuesday decreed a state of national emergency and imposed press censorship ahead of a one-day general strike called by left-wing trade unions for today. An official communique said the emergency made the whole territory a security zone, with the army in charge of public order.'
– Financial Times 2.6.88

'Against a background of labour unrest, Prime Minister Turgat Ozal . . . ruled out any immediate wage increases for workers . . . The current account deficit dropped by 35% in 1987 to $987 million due to increased exports.'
– Dayanisma, Turkish Solidarity Campaign Newsletter, January 1986

(left) Demonstration in Chile against torture, later dispersed with tear gas. *(Chile Solidarity Campaign) (above)* Chilean police arrest demonstrators.

Rich-poor gap widens

The gap between rich and poor now widens. Many people who used to scrape by, can barely afford to feed themelves these days. Meanwhile those who have 'made it' – the big landowners, senior civil servants, army officers and the handful of managers in the foreign-owned factories – continue to enjoy a high standard of living. However, economic forecasts look bleak and the well-off classes begin to feel nervous about the demonstrations and strikes which threaten to destroy their tenuous economic security. At a time of sluggish business and sinking world prices for coffee and tobacco, they are less and less willing to share their wealth. On the contrary, rich families now start barring their windows and hiring security guards. They donate money to private armies to defend their interests and put pressure on the government to step up law and order.

Military repression

The military and para-military forces are then expanded and armed with newly imported weaponry, while foreign advisors (from one of the superpowers, for example) with a stake in the country come to advise them on counter-insurgency. A number of repressive tactics are now adopted in order to silence opposition: curfews are imposed, political detainees are tortured and villages thought to be sympathetic to popular guerilla forces are razed to the ground. Cosmetic attempts at reform are doomed to failure because the situation has now become so polarised.

Military coup and more arms imports

Eventually the existing civilian government is ousted and replaced by a military-dominated grouping. As economic instability worsens, another

Police patrol in wealthy suburb, Guatemala city. Notice the high-security wall behind. *(Mike Goldwater/Network).*

loan is obtained on the understanding that law and order will be maintained and foreign business interests protected. This time a military aid package forms part of the loan agreement, resulting in massive orders with foreign arms companies for new armaments, including tanks and fighter aircraft.

Arms race

One result of this is an increase in arms purchases by two neighbouring countries as they observe the continuing militarisation of country X. The groundwork for a local arms race has been laid.

Arms and poverty

At this point armaments represent 30% of all imports and the government spends more on the armed forces than on education or health. Such heavy military spending depresses productivity and aggravates inflation. As popular discontent increases, so too does repression and hence the volume of arms imports designed to artificially bolster the military regime's fragile power. A vicious cycle of poverty, repression and militarisation is now well and truly underway.

Conclusion

By adding to Third World governments' debt problems, arms imports are indirectly responsible for the drastic cash-generating policies introduced to pay back the debts. These policies range from removing food subsidies to cutting wages or stepping up cash crop farming, but nearly all of them hit the poor hardest. At the same time, arms imports contribute to the militarisation of the governments concerned – governments which have become more and more divorced from the majority interests of the population. When people protest at the policies instituted to pay back the debt, the State often responds with violent repression. The resulting insecurity is used as an excuse for buying yet more arms. And so the cycle goes on.

NOTES

1: See Robin Luckham: 'Militarism and International Dependence' in *Disarmament and World Development* ed. Richard Jolly (Pergamon Press, 1978).

CHAPTER 7

Indonesia – A vicious cycle

To add a more true-to-life dimension to the Poverty-Repression-Militarisation cycle, there follows a case-study of events in Indonesia, a major customer for British weapons.

Background

Straddling some of the world's major sea routes and rich in natural resources, Indonesia has always figured prominently in international economics. In 1000 AD, Asian traders were already selling their wares in these islands and by the sixteenth and seventeenth centuries, Dutch and Portugese colonists were grappling for control of the lucrative 'Spice Islands'. Today Indonesia is a honeypot for multinational corporations and a lynchpin of western military strategy. In view of its importance, it was almost inevitable that Indonesia's history would be one of upheaval and exploitation.

Dutch colony

From the early seventeenth century until 1949, most of the 13,000 islands which constitute modern Indonesia were under Dutch colonial rule. During this period, a pattern was set in motion which altered little even after independence in 1949. It was a pattern in which the natural resources of Indonesia were plundered largely for foreign profit, with a small local elite also benefitting, while the great majority of the people lived in poverty. Profits from the export of Indonesian cash crops eventually came to supply a third of the total Dutch government budget. The level of exploitation worsened towards the end of the nineteenth century when the Dutch authorities permitted private Dutch individuals to purchase Indonesian land.

After independence

Indonesia's islands contain a blending of every culture that ever invaded them – Chinese, Indian, Melanesian, Portugese, Polynesian, Arabian, English and Dutch. Literally hundreds of local languages and dialects are spoken. In a country with such ethnic diversity, the concept of belonging to a unified political whole is still a new one. This may explain why Sukarno, the first Indonesian president after Independence, centred his

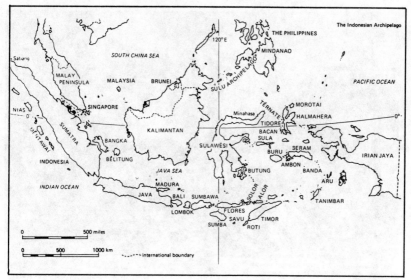

Archipelago of Indonesia.

domestic policies on the promotion of national unity and identity. Yet, given the country's fragmented nature and the economic dislocation caused by colonialism, Sukarno had a hard task on his hands. Little attention was given to economic problems, with the result that inflation soared, exports fell, and foreign indebtedness rose, not least because of the high military spending of the armed forces.

During this period the anti-Sukarno army leadership became increasingly powerful, boosted by arms, military advisors and money from the US government. Opposed to President Sukarno and his Indonesian nationalism, the US wished to install an elite of US-trained bureaucrats and military personnel who would support and implement its own 'strategic' designs for Indonesia.

Military dictatorship

By the mid 1960s, government inability to grapple with domestic problems had led to growing conflicts between the armed forces and the political parties, particularly the Indonesian Communist Party (PKI). This culminated in a murder strike against the army's General Staff, engineered by a General Suharto, but ostensibly launched by a group of rebel army officers. With most of the army behind him, Suharto took steps to put down this so-called 'coup attempt' and then manoeuvred himself into a position where Sukarno had to cede extensive powers to

Military coup, 1966

him. The PKI with three million members at this point was now blamed for the 'coup attempt', giving Suharto an excuse to launch a massive backlash against PKI members and known sympathisers. Between October 1965 and March 1966, around a *million* people were killed and thousands more imprisoned. In the meantime, Suharto organised a successful coup, taking full control of the armed forces and the security apparatus. By March 1966, Sukarno had surrendered all his powers to Suharto, leading eventually to Suharto's appointment as full president in 1968. He has ruled Indonesia ever since.

Political repression

Suharto's power continues to emanate from the army, as reflected in the number of ex-army officers occupying senior positions in the civil service and state-controlled businesses. This military oligarchy has striven to eliminate all opposition, imprisoning and torturing tens of thousands of people over the past twenty years. Newspapers and books which criticise the regime have been banned, and trade unions crushed. The repression and bloodshed for which Suharto's regime is responsible puts it on a par with the Idi Amin regime in Uganda or the Pol Pot regime in Kampuchea. Yet while these despots have been overthrown, Suharto's regime lives on, under the economic and political patronage of the western industrialised powers.

One major aspect of this patronage has been the sale of military equipment which still flows into Indonesia, particularly from the US and western Europe, despite the brutality for which the Indonesian military are responsible. This flow of arms has been very marked since the late 1970s when the US doubled its arms trade with Indonesia and massively increased military aid to the Suharto regime following Communist victories in Vietnam.

Uneven development

In the economic sphere, the military regime's policies have been equally unjust. Soon after seizing power in the 1960s, Suharto turned to a group of US-trained economic technocrats, supposedly to redirect the economy. There was little that was new in their approach. As in colonial times, economic recipes were based on the exploitation of Indonesia's natural resources, particularly petroleum, but also timber and minerals. The foreign exchange generated from exporting these raw materials was used to finance the country's further development. By the beginning of the 1980s, Indonesia's economy could boast huge foreign exchange reserves, burgeoning oil exploration and the world's largest exports of liquid natural gas. Yet, despite these successes, the purchasing power of the poorest 40% of the population had declined by an average of 24% since 1970 and today average living standards are amongst the lowest in Asia.[1]

Indonesian prison

Divided country
(above) Modern street,
Jakarta
*(Jenny Matthews/
Format)*

(left) Weeding rice
(Jenny Matthews/Format)

INDONESIA – THE FACTS

Population:	175 million. 75% of the population is rural.
Daily per capita calorie supply:	2,476 – fractionally above the minimum requirement, 45% of the population are living on less than 1,900 calories a day.
Infant mortality:	88 per 1000 die before the age of one (10 per 1000 in Britain).
Doctors per person:	1:12,330 (1:729 in Britain). Only 25% of babies and 5% of children under 5 have access to public health centres.
Access to safe drinking water:	33% of the population.
Life expectancy:	55 years (74 in Britain).
Land:	Of the 130 million people in rural areas, over 40 million are landless; 46 million own no more than 0.25 hectares.
Literacy:	74% (99% in Britain). 63% of children of school age (5–19) attend school but at least 25% of those who have completed primary school are still illiterate.
Unemployment and underemployment:	30–40%.

Sources
Asia Yearbook 1988; World Development Report 1988; *World Military and Social Expenditures 1987/88*.

Development statistics point to the existence of a dual economy in Indonesia. On the one hand, there is a foreign-owned exports sector servicing the factories of the industrialised world and a local elite which lives in the lap of luxury. On the other hand, there is the vast majority of people, at least 70% of whom are caught in an all-too-familiar cycle of poverty, malnutrition and disease. For them, the so-called 'economic miracle' of Indonesia's recovery might as well never have happened. Indeed, many of the policies promoted by Suharto have been at the expense of the poor. An increased output of cash crops like rubber, coffee and palm oil, for example, has involved the expansion of cash crop farms. Smallholdings previously owned by peasant farmers have been swallowed up in this process, thereby swelling the ranks of under-employed landless labourers. These peasant people have either drifted to the shanty areas of the cities or have accepted government resettlement in the outer islands on land belonging to local tribal people. One group of oppressed people is thus being pitted against another.

Miracle short-lived

But even for the rich minority, their economic position is far from secure. The policy of pinning the country's wealth on the export of raw materials has proved a dubious gamble. By the early 1980s, 70% of Indonesia's export earnings and 60% of its revenues came from oil.[2] Thus when oil prices started to fall in the mid-1980s, Indonesia was suddenly hit by a major financial crisis. Between January and September 1986, the price of a barrel of oil fell from $25 to $13 and by the end of the fiscal year 1986–87, Indonesia's income from oil had been halved.[3]

Western aid

The effects of this economic crisis have been far-reaching. By the end of 1988, Indonesia's foreign debt stood at $50 billion and in 1987 the interest payments on this debt absorbed 41% of its export earnings.[4] Indonesia has only narrowly avoided bankruptcy by turning to powerful financial institutions in Japan and the West to tide it over. In 1986 the Inter-Govermental Group on Indonesia (IGGI) which meets annually to fix the West's aid commitment to Indonesia, granted a sum of $2.5 billion to be transferred in the form of bilateral aid, soft loans and export credits. Under this agreement, Britain put up £140 million in soft loans to prevent British companies, including arms manufacturers, from losing business with Indonesia, currently Britain's sixth largest 'trading partner'.

Yet the vast sum allocated in 1986 proved insufficient and when the IGGI met in 1988 it granted a further record sum of $5.7 billion to aid the ailing Indonesian economy. This is expected to cover 70% of the development budget and more than 25% of total spending, reflecting the extent to which Indonesia is now *dependent* on foreign aid.

Economic cutbacks and more arms purchases

Creditors in the West have made it clear that this aid is only granted on the condition that the Indonesian government make yet more concessions to foreign companies and introduce a series of austerity measures in the public sector. This has further reduced living standards amongst the population. In 1986, spending on priority areas such as education, agriculture, communications and rural development was cut by up to 25%.[5]

Yet, almost in the same breath, Suharto's generals announced their intention to buy 12 F-16 fighter jets from the US and agreed to purchase a further batch of British Aerospace Rapier missiles at a cost of £40 million. Meanwhile, Indonesia's own fledgling arms industry has continued to grow in collaboration with western arms companies. In March 1987, *Jane's Defence Weekly* observed that 'despite budget cuts and the impact of devaluation, the military industries seem to have been encouraged to expand.'[6] With military officers holding the reins of power in Indonesia, the preferences of the military sector are granted at the expense of the civilian population.

Protest meets with repression

The impact of the debt crisis and the Government's austerity measures have resulted in a growing undercurrent of unrest. In February 1989, for example, hundreds of university students demonstrated in Central Java against the 'strong arm tactics' used by the Government to remove families from the Kedong Ombo region for a World Bank dam project.[7] However the tight grip of the security forces on society continues

Indonesian army represses a demonstration

to block any open expression of protest. The student movement is prevented from creating their own independent organisations, following a crackdown on student protests in 1978. Muslim activists have also become the target of state repression. In 1984, the army opened fire on a Muslim demonstration in Jakarta's dockland, killing dozens, possibly hundreds of people. In 1989 at least thirty people were killed when Indonesian troops attacked Moslem protestors in South Sumatra. Tens of thousands of former political prisoners arrested in the late 1960s still suffer widespread abuse of their civil rights.

British armoured car used against student demonstration

Indonesian expansionism

Meanwhile the Suharto regime is in the business of brutally expanding Indonesian territory. In 1962 West Papua was occupied and in December 1975 the Indonesian armed forces launched a full-scale invasion of the former Portugese colony, East Timor. Since then, East Timor has been the scene of untold attrocities leading to the death of 200,000 people. This war is discussed in more detail in the following chapter.

British arms trade with Indonesia

The cycle of repression and poverty in Indonesia is likely to go on, so long as the Indonesian armed forces continue to be reinforced with western arms, including some from Britain. Regardless of the appalling human rights record of the Indonesian armed forces, the British Government has issued licences to British arms companies to supply Indonesia with a vast array of military equipment ranging from warships and combat aircraft to armoured vehicles and missile launchers.

This trade first took off in a big way in 1978 when the then Labour Government authorised the sale of eight British Aerospace Hawk ground attack aircraft to Indonesia. At that time the Indonesian armed forces were waging war in East Timor and as a result there was widespread

(top) Hawk aircraft
(above) Rapier missile

protest against the Hawk deal. Nevertheless, the deal went ahead amidst claims from the Foreign Secretary, David Owen, that 'the scale of the fighting (in East Timor) . . . has been very greatly reduced'[8] and that the Hawks were only trainer models, despite proof to the contrary.[9]

British Aerospace in the forefront

Once Mrs Thatcher entered office in 1979, the British arms trade to Indonesia grew in leaps and bounds, with British Aerospace remaining in the forefront of this trade. Indonesia now has twenty Hawk aircraft, enough to equip two combat squadrons. In fact it is now thought that British Aerospace has offered to co-operate with Indonesia's state-owned aerospace industry, IPTN, in building Hawk HS-200 aircraft on location in Indonesia. Not satisfied with its Hawk sales, in 1986 British Aerospace was reported to be bidding to sell the supersonic Tornado aircraft to Indonesia.

Determined to consolidate its military collaboration with the Suharto regime, British Aerospace is also supplying the Indonesian armed forces with Rapier ground-to-air missiles, having concluded three consecutive contracts worth a total of £340 million. The deals include offset benefits, allocating part of the manufacturing of the missiles to IPTN. In order to train Indonesian army personnel in the use of these missiles, a special British Aerospace technical college has been constructed on the island of Java.

Support for the Indonesian Navy

Britain has sold a large range of naval equipment to the Indonesian Navy. During 1985 and 1986, three Tribal-class frigates refurbished at the Vosper Thorneycroft shipyards, were supplied as well as a naval survey ship. The latter can be equipped with weapons, as was shown during the Falklands War when similar vessels carried weapons. The British Government has also issued licences for the export of Seawolf missile launchers.

Visits

Military co-operation between the two countries has been reinforced by a constant stream of official visits to and from Indonesia. In 1987, for example, Britain was graced with visits from Dr. B.J. Habibie, Indonesian Minister of Research and Technology, Dr Suleiman Wiria-didaja, from the Indonesian Shipbuilding Organisation, and General Tri Sutrisno, now Commander-in-Chief of the Indonesian Armed Forces. British officials visiting Indonesia in 1987 included the Vice Chief of Defence Staff and Tim Sainsbury MP, Under-Secretary for Defence

Mrs Thatcher with President Suharto, 1985

Procurement. In April 1985, Mrs Thatcher herself paid a visit to Indonesia, during which she made no secret of the fact that collaboration in military affairs was high on her agenda. Indeed, the highlight of her stay in Indonesia was a visit to the Nurtanio aircraft factory, the centre-piece of Indonesia's military-industrial complex.

Training

Indonesian military personnel receive extensive training from British armed forces both in Britain and on location in Indonesia.

Motives

British arms exports to Indonesia are now worth tens of millions of pounds a year and are therefore very lucrative to British arms companies. However, there is another more deep-seated motive behind the British Government's promotion of arms sales to Indonesia, as revealed in official Foreign Office communiques:

'In considering export licence applications for the sale of defence equipment . . . we cannot overlook Indonesia's role as an important regional power in South East Asia. The security and stability in Indonesia is of growing significance to the international community, not least to Britain which has substantial interests there.'[10]

These interests include investments which are estimated to be in the region of £600 million, excluding British finance that reaches the country through Hongkong and Singapore-based ventures. Selling weapons is thus perceived by Mrs Thatcher's Government as a means of protecting British and western economic interests in the region. The Government implicitly assumes that any threat to these interests should be countered by the Indonesian authorities, using military force.

Conclusion

Economic and political dislocation – the legacies of colonialism – and growing US interference in the country's internal affairs paved the way for military rule in Indonesia under President Suharto. During his two decades in power, Suharto has transformed Indonesia into one of the most repressive countries in the world. In this he has been greatly aided by the continuous flow of arms from western countries, including Britain. Policies intended to modernise Indonesia such as the expansion of a cash crop economy and the investment of state funds in high-tech weapons and military industry, have largely been at the expense of the general population whose living standards remain very poor. As Indonesia has fallen deeper into debt, it is the poorer sectors of the population who have suffered most from the austerity measures advocated by Indonesia's foreign creditors. So long as the Suharto regime can repress internal disent and enlist the support of the major western powers, it will no doubt continue to carry out such policies.

NOTES
1: Figures quoted in 'Profile Indonesia' pamphlet, CAFOD/CIIR, 1981.
2: *Financial Times* 8.1.86.
3: Op. cit. 17.9.86.
4: Op. cit. 2.6.87 and 20.5.88.
5: Op. cit. 8.1.86.
6: *Jane's Defence Weekly* 14.3.87.
7: Reported in *The Guardian* 28.2.89.
8: Letter from David Owen to Lord Avebury, 19.6.78.
9: See chapter 9 for evidence that Hawk aircraft exported to Indonesia were combat/trainer models.
10: Letter from the Foreign Office 11.5.87.

We are indebted to TAPOL, the Indonesian human rights organisation, for the background material in this chapter. For more information, contact: TAPOL, 111 Northwood Road, Thornton Heath, Surrey, CR4 8HW. Tel. 01–771 2904.

CHAPTER 8

Britain and repressive technology

Advertisement
for British
CS gas
anti-riot guns

The Indonesian government is just one of some thirty governmental customers of British weapons listed by Amnesty International as major human rights violators.[1] A considerable proportion of the military equipment exported to these repressive governments is used *directly* to suppress human rights and internal dissent. Such equipment is broadly referred to as 'repressive technology'. While it includes items such as leg-irons and electric shock prods, this category also extends to the whole apparatus of repression: riot-control gear, armoured vehicles, ground-attack aircraft, machine guns and other small arms, ammunition, police

RUC arrest, Northern Ireland, a testing ground for repressive technology
(Laurie Sparham, Network)

computers, Land Rovers, surveillance devices and training in the use of internal security equipment. It is estimated that the trade in repressive technology accounts for 10–20% of the total value of the arms trade.[2]

The chief suppliers of repressive technology correspond closely to the major arms exporters. Top of the list is the United States, infamous for its role in equipping the notorious armed forces of El Salvador and Guatemala (amongst others) with enormous quantities of hardware for systematic and brutal repression. But Britain also has a major stake in the repression trade. In fact its arms companies are widely acclaimed for their expertise in repressive technology, reflecting Britain's history of supporting unpopular elites (many of them in ex-British colonies) and the experience gained by British troops and security forces in Northern Ireland. Much of the equipment tried and tested in the six counties since the late 1960s, such as armoured cars, water cannon, CS gas, rubber and plastic bullets, and surveillance equipment, is now routinely exported.

Not just weapons of repression

The Foreign Office has conceded that it will not permit the export to countries such as Chile and Indonesia of any items which 'in our judgement, are likely to be used for internal repression'.[3] When the sale of overtly repressive equipment is in the offing, it would appear that the Government *does* pay attention to human rights. Less likely to be blocked are sales to repressive governments of 'dual use' equipment such as computers, Land Rovers, and telecommunications systems – equipment which has civilian uses but which can also be used to suppress human rights.

The Government's lax attitude towards dual use equipment enabled telephone-tapping systems and surveillance radios to be legally supplied to the Ugandan Idi Amin regime in the 1970s, despite its appalling human rights record. Britain continues to transfer dual use repression hardware to South Africa, despite the UN arms embargo. In 1978 two ICL computers were sold to the South African police, one of their reputed uses being the administration of apartheid pass laws. The main four-wheel drive vehicle deployed by the South African security forces is the Land Rover which was exported from Britain at least until 1985–86. These vehicles were used during the 1976 Soweto demonstrations in which a hundred young demonstrators were killed by the South African

Land Rovers have been exported to South Africa. *(Rover – Triumph)*

army.[4] In 1987 Philips two-way radios were sold to the Chilean police with the excuse that they were to be used for crowd control during the Pope's visit. There has been considerable speculation as to the application of this equipment *since* the Pope's visit: Chilean police have been photographed at demonstrations with two-way radios.[5]

Arms intended primarily for defence against *external* forces, such as fighter aircraft, warships or sophisticated missiles, have also been transferred with British government approval to repressive regimes. These exports may seem far removed from torture equipment but serve equally well in strengthening the hand of repressive governments. Fighter aircraft, for example, while unlikely to be used directly for internal repression, are regarded by many governments – particularly military ones – as symbols of power and prestige. In so bolstering the morale of repressive governments, exports of major weapon systems undermine the cause of those struggling for peace and justice in these countries, as confirmed by the various opposition groups concerned. The President of the National Trade Union Committee of Chile writes: 'It is extremely important that pressure is brought to bear on the British government to cut off *all* arms supplies to Chile.' (our emphasis)[6]

Training for repression

Weapons are not the only British commodity exported to repressive regimes. In addition, training is provided free of charge by British armed forces to military personnel from a large number of repressive governments under a special Foreign Office aid programme.[7] Whatever the nature of the training, the mere offer of this service to a government's armed forces is often interpreted as a sign of British support for the government concerned. Following a visit to El Salvador in 1986, for example, George Foulkes MP claimed that the military training programme undertaken at Sandhurst military college by a Salvadorean army officer earlier that year was viewed by the Salvadorean Defence Minister as representing British approval of his government.[8]

Considering that the Salvadorean armed forces are engaged in bombing rural villages and many of the Salvadorean officers are suspected death squad organisers, there is legitimate concern over the sort of training foreign armed forces are receiving in Britain. A visitor to Sandhurst in 1987 claimed that a Sri Lankan officer, on being asked what he was going to do when he got back to his country, replied, 'Kill Tamils' – the Tamils being the minority ethnic group within the predominantly Sinhalese population of Sri Lanka.[9] Whether this officer's resolve reflected the training he had just received cannot be verified, as the British government does not disclose details on this issue.

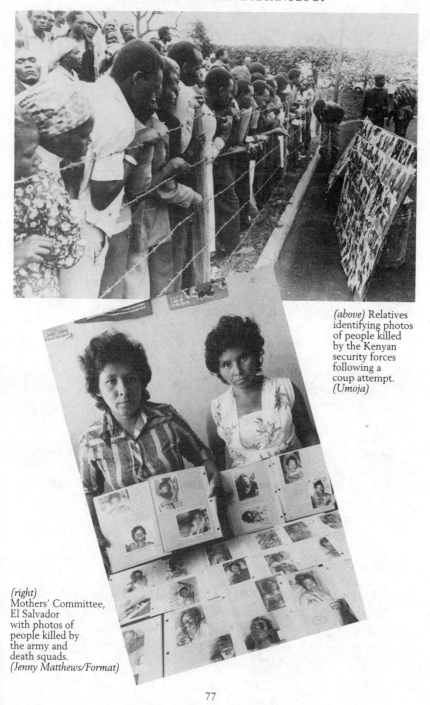

(above) Relatives identifying photos of people killed by the Kenyan security forces following a coup attempt. (Umoja)

(right) Mothers' Committee, El Salvador with photos of people killed by the army and death squads. (Jenny Matthews/Format)

CUSTOMERS OF BRITISH REPRESSIVE TECHNOLOGY

Kenya

Wanjiru Kihoro, a Kenyan economist, has claimed that 'with the support of its powerful backers (including Britain) the Kenyan regime has become more confident of its ability to repress democratic dissent.'[10] Following an attempted coup in 1982, an estimated 2,000 people were killed by US- and British-trained security forces. In 1984 the same security forces massacred at least 1,400 civilians in the Wajir district. In 1986/87 over 300 people were arrested for alleged opposition to the Government. Of these, some have since 'disappeared' while others have been tortured and ill-treated.

Chile

On 11th September 1973, the democratically elected government of Salavador Allende was overthrown by Chilean armed forces in a coup characterised by the murder, torture and detention of thousands of people. The new military junta led by General Pinochet stopped all elections, closed down the Congress, and introduced a hardline monetarist economic policy which has thrown millions of Chileans into poverty. Although international pressure has had some effect, human rights violations continue on a massive scale. Despite this, Britain renewed arms sales to the Pinochet dictatorship in 1980 and is now a major supplier of the Chilean armed forces (partly because the United States has imposed an embargo on military trade with Chile).

British weapons sold to Chile since 1979 include: naval ships, ground attack aircraft, bomber aircraft, Exocet-type missiles, Seacat missiles, Blowpipe missiles, and radio communications equipment. Entensive training is also provided for Chilean military personnel.[11]

Ex-Royal Navy destroyers have been sold to the Chilean Navy, despite the fact that naval ships are known to have been used as prisons and torture centres (although there is no proof that ex-British ships have been used in this way). In 1984 Chile was considering purchasing the British AMAC riot control vehicle until public protest forced the British Government to block the sale. However this did not prevent Britain from discussing the sale of the British Centaur half-track vehicle to Chile in 1985, even though a similar vehicle was used on the streets of Santiago in August 1983 to crush opposition protests.[12] During these protests, 31 people were killed and hundreds wounded.

Women coughing on CS gas, Chile.

Photograph by Julio Etchart

Police with radios arrest a journalist in Chile. Britain has sold radios to the Chilean police.

Conclusion

Britain is amongst the world's leading exporters of repressive technology and has therefore made a major contribution to the military repression of thousands of people in the Third World today. But even military exports with no obvious repressive application can encourage further human rights violations, if only by legitimising the regimes concerned.

NOTES

1: Out of the 74 countries which attended the British Army Equipment Exhibition in 1986, 30 were countries which had been named in the major Amnesty International report, *Torture in the Eighties*, A.I. Publications, 1984.
2: See Michael T. Klare and Cynthia Arnson: 'Supplying Repression: US Support for Authoritarian Regimes Abroad'.
3: Letter from the Foreign Office to CAAT, 20.9.84.
4: See CAAT briefing on South Africa (1988) for more information.
5: See photograph in *Oxfam News*, Summer 1987.
6: Quoted at the time of the threatened sale of the AMAC riot control vehicle to Chile in 1984.
7: See chapter 3 for more details on training aid offered by the British Government to foreign military personnel.
8: See George Foulkes in Hansard 15.12.86. See also chapter 9 for more information on El Salavador.
9: Letter to *The Guardian* 12.3.87.
10: Wanjiru Kihoro in *Sanity* September 1985.
11: See CAAT leaflet on arms sales to Chile.
12: The sale of Centaur half-track vehicles to Chile was under negotiation in 1985.

CHAPTER 9
Fuel of war

Contrary to claims that there has been peace for forty years [1], war has erupted on 120 occasions around the world since 1945, resulting in the death of over 30 million people.[2] This is something like four times as many war-related deaths as in the period 1900 to 1940. During 1987 alone, there were 36 wars raging in different parts of the world, nearly all of which were in the Third World.[3] In fact, of the wars to have taken place since World War II, 99% have been in the Third World.

Role of the arms trade

Despite the indifference of our government to many of the wars now going on in the Third World, Britain is implicated in a large proportion of these conflicts, however far away they may seem. After all, nearly all the weaponry for such wars has been supplied by industrialised countries like Britain. It is no accident that the sharp rise in casualty figures for regional wars since the early part of this century has co-incided with a massive expansion in the arms trade.

To suggest that the arms trade is the root cause of these wars would be an over-simplification. However, it is certain that the transfer of vast quantities of weapons to Third World countries has served to fuel conflict by aggravating political tensions, blocking attempts at peaceful solutions and raising the threshold of violence. Most Third World countries lack the facilities to produce anything other than small arms and ammunition. Only by importing sophisticated weapons and technology from the industrialised countries have warring parties been able to fight such large-scale wars. This means that the arms trade bears a high degree of responsibility for the violence and destruction caused by recent wars.

Modern warfare

Of the wars to have taken place since 1945, only 15% have involved the armies of two or more countries fighting each other across borders. The other 85% have come about through the attempted overthrow of central governments (many of them colonial) or as a result of tensions erupting *within* countries such as ethnic and religious differences or social inequalities.[4] Although external powers such as the US or the USSR have intervened on a number of occasions, most of these wars have been *internal*. Invariably they are wars in which the armed forces of the ruling central government confront a guerilla army operating in rural areas within the country's borders.

In this situation, the concept of two opposing armies occasionally meeting to do battle with each other is outmoded. Increasingly it is civilians – and not armies – who make up the largest number of casualties, partly because of the internal nature of such conflicts. In many cases, civilians may sympathise with, or actively assist, one or other side in the war. This being the case, suspected civilian collaborators are usually regarded as targets by the enemy forces. Even if local populations endeavour to remain detached from such events, they invariably find themselves caught in the crossfire.

Civilian casualties

The rise in civilian deaths is the most alarming trend in modern warfare. Looking at the casualty figures for World War I (1914–18), we find that 95% of the deaths were military; yet, by contrast, during the Vietnam War (1960–75), 80% of the casualties were civilian.[5] In the case of wars fought in the 1980s, civilians accounted for a staggering 85% of recorded deaths.[6] 'Civilians have always suffered in times of war,' writes journalist Brian Walker. 'But at least (in the past) there was recognition that the innocent *ought* not to suffer. Today little or no attempt is made to protect them.'[7] This is a fact which military strategists also admit. In 1986, the US Under Secretary of Defense, Fred C. Ikle, observed: 'Today one out of every four countries around the globe is at war. These are not wars . . . where armies roll across borders, (or) where hundreds of air-craft fight for control of the skies. Rather, they are insurgent and local conflicts in which people get killed . . . by grenades, bullets, mines (and) bombs dropped from aircraft.'[8]

This development has turned the arms trade into a particularly nasty business. Put bluntly, it means that Britain and other arms-producing countries are selling weapons to kill unarmed civilians, most of whom have probably taken no part in the fighting.

Effects of war

In addition to those killed and wounded, homes, factories, warehouses, whole towns and acres of farming land are destroyed by war. Thousands are left homeless and dislocated from their communities. Civilians who find themselves living on a battleground can often only escape the fighting by fleeing from their homes. This may explain why there are now as many as eight million refugees worldwide, mostly women and children, who have been displaced as a result of war.[9] Quite apart from the social and psychological distress caused, displacement also holds grave demographic implications. While laying waste to some regions, mass evacuations place pressure on other regions, creating food shortages. This may be aggravated by an acute shortage of labour in rural areas owing to the number of agricultural workers engaged in fighting. Since 70% of the population of the Third World is dependent on farming, the effect of war on land is very serious. Equally serious is the huge expense to governments of waging modern warfare. In many cases, public funds are drained to such an extent that even the most basic needs of the population such as food and shelter can no longer be met.

British complicity – the facts

Glossy military adverts and government propaganda portray British weapons as though they were as innocuous as household appliances. The carnage which they can cause is discreetly hidden behind respectable adjectives like 'advanced', 'effective' and 'technological'. No reference is made to the fact that Britains's military customers actually *use* this equipment to kill and harm peple. Thus, in order to bring the relationship between war and the arms trade into sharper focus, there follow some reports of conflict in countries which Britain has recently supplied with weapons and brief details of the British equipment sold to these countries.

Turkey

The Turkish armed forces have been involved in a longstanding and repressive campaign against Kurdish guerilla groups demanding self-determination from Turkey. Meanwhile Britain's military trade with Turkey has seen a steep rise since September 1980. Weapons recently sold include: 36 Rapier surface-to-air missiles; gun barrels for tanks; an Aptitude Testing system for pilots; 400 military Land Rovers; Sea Skua anti-ship missiles. Turkey is now considering the purchase of 30 Tornado fighter aircraft from British Aerospace worth £500 million. Members of the Turkish armed forces also receive training from the British armed forces.

'Turkish planes yesterday attacked three villages in northern Iraq which Ankara claimed were separatist guerilla bases (of the Kurdish Workers' Party) from which recent terrorist attacks into eastern Turkey have been launched. An unconfirmed news agency report said 100 rebels were killed ... About 30 aircraft were used to bomb camps ...' – The Guardian 5.3.87

Military advertisements say nothing of the effects of the weapons.

Afghanistan

Despite attempts at a ceasefire, war was still raging in Afghanistan in 1988. Blowpipe shoulder-fired missiles manufactured by Short Brothers of Belfast have been supplied in large quantities to the anti-Soviet Afghan resistance, Mujahedin, fighting the Afghan and occupying Soviet armed forces. The Mujahedin received its first consignment in the spring of 1986 and for a full six months the Blowpipe was by far the most sophisticated weapon in the guerilla armoury. It is thought that the British Government specifically authorised sales of Blowpipe to the United States in the knowledge that they would be funnelled into the huge CIA arms pipeline through Pakistan to the Afghan guerillas. There have been claims that they were supplied to the US from Ministry of Defence stockpiles.[10]

'If and when peace is achieved, dispossessed families will return to a devastated countryside incapable of feeding them. Crop yields are down by an average of 40% rising to 80% in some regions, an agricultural nightmare that spells continuing dependence on outside aid ... More than 12,000 of Afghanistan's 22,000 farming villages have been destroyed or abandoned ... It will take 8–9 years to regenerate herds of sheep, goats and cattle ...' – The Observer 27.3.88

Morocco

Since 1976, King Hassan of Morocco has attempted to occupy the Western Sahara by force, following a declaration of independence by the region's inhabitants, the Sahwari people. There has been heavy fighting between Morocco and the Sahwari army, Polisario, which has culminated in Morocco's construction of a 2,000 km wall enclosing virtually the whole Western Sahara region. Aerial bombardment of Sahwari camps by King Hassan's forces has been a common feature of the war. Despite recent negotiations over a ceasefire, the fighting was continuing in 1988.

The Moroccan military are equipped with British artillery equipment, some of which has been photographed in action in the Western Sahara.[11] During a visit to Britain in 1987, King Hassan was introduced to a number of representatives from British arms companies and it is thought discussions touched upon Vickers tanks and EMI radars. Ironically, in 1983 the Government Export Credit Guarantee Department announced that it would provide £500 million worth of credit for military contracts with Algeria, Polisario's major supplier of arms.

'A series of Moroccan air strikes, using cluster bombs, phosphorous and napalm, drove the refugees on into neighbouring Algeria. Many people

Sahwari people who face Moroccan military aggression *(War on Want)*

were killed or wounded and refugees still remember the horrifying casualties. Younger refugees now evoke the flight of the Sahwaris in their paintings of women and children fleeing as bombs fall around them.' – Exiles of the Sahara by James Firebrace. War on Want 1987

Sudan

Throughout 1988 a brutal war was being fought in the south of Sudan between pro-Sudanese government forces and the Sudan People's Liberation Army. In 1983 Sudan ordered 10 trainer/counter-insurgency aircraft from British Aerospace, three of which were delivered in 1984. Further deliveries were then halted owing to the Sudanese government's financial difficulties. It is likely that the three counter-insurgency planes have been used in military operations in the south of the country. Britain's complicity in this war has been fortified by extensive training provided for Sudanese army officers.

'Thousands of civilians have been massacred by militias backing the Sudanese government in its fight against rebels in southern Sudan ... The Minority Rights Group said the five-year conflict between government forces and the Sudan People's Liberation Army had also destroyed rural economies, caused famine and displaced hundreds of thousands of people.' – The Guardian 6.5.88

Southern Africa

As part of a strategy to destabilise the independent black African states on its borders, South African forces occupied large areas of southern Angola until August 1988 and continue to direct and supply Unita, a guerilla army waging war against the Angolan government. In 1988 South Africa was still illegally occupying Namibia with military force and was funding and training brutal anti-government groups in Mozambique (MNR) and Lesotho (LLA).

The backbone of this war machine is western military equipment, some of it British. Despite the UN embargo on arms sales to South Africa, a large amount of British military equipment has been legally exported to South Africa, including military radar systems, computers and Land Rovers. This is largely due to the gaping loophole in Britain's interpretation of the arms embargo which means that only the export of equipment 'specifically designed for military use' is banned. This narrow definition has permitted the export of 'dual use' equipment – items which have a possible civilian application, as well as a military one. Many British companies, such as ICL, GEC/Marconi and Plessey also have subsidiary companies in South Africa.[12]

Houses bombed by
South African forces,
Angola *(War on Want)*

Mozambican child whose feet
were blown off by an MNR landmine
(Mike Goldwater/Network)

'Scarce resources have been channelled into the (Angolan) armed forces, fighting successive South African attacks in the south and the Unita guerilla war which has spread over 90% of the country. Agriculture has been ravaged, trade and transport disrupted and last year, $1.15 billion, 34% of total government expenditure was spent on defence and security.' – Financial Times 4.8.86.

'In 1982, when I was just 10 years old, I lived with my family in a village in Mozambique. All the villages are in danger from the MNR, and no one knows when they might attack. One day the MNR came to our village. We heard the gunfire and tried to run away. As we ran, two of my brothers were shot. I was very frightened. We had to hide until we thought it was safe to return to the village. There we found many people dead, and many houses destroyed.' – Angelino Dando, Mozambique, quoted by Save the Children Fund, Autumn 1988.

East Timor

As shown in chapter 7, the primary function of the Indonesian armed forces is to maintain internal security [13] but in addition to this they are also involved in ruthlessly expanding Indonesian territory. In 1962 West Papua was occupied and in December 1975 came the turn of East Timor.

Until 1975, the eastern side of the island of Timor had remained a Portuguese colony. But in the early seventies, nationalism began to gather force in East Timor. Following the revolution in Portugal, the Portuguese abruptly withdrew from the territory, paving the way for an independent East Timorese government led by the Fretilin party. For three short months the people of East Timor were able to determine their own destiny. Yet this was not to last. Indonesia's President Suharto, feeling threatened by a small progressive nation on his borders that might inspire other secessionist movements within the country, ordered his armed forces to invade East Timor. The resulting war on the island has been marked by extreme barbarity and violence on the part of the occupying Indonesian forces. Conservative estimates put the number of people killed in the first few years of occupation at around 200,000 which is approximatly one third of the original population. In their attempt to annihilate the Fretilin resistance, Indonesian military personnel have continued to launch major offensives on East Timor, destroying crops, homes and villages through systematic bombing. Many communities have been herded into 'strategic villages' which operate like prisons.

(right) Indonesian planes dropping bombs on East Timor

East Timorese children

Britain is a major supplier of weapons and technology to Indonesia, as already explained in chapter 7. For example, the Indonesian air force now has 20 British Aerospace Hawk aircraft. While the British government claims the Hawks are only trainers, British Aerospace itself describes the particular model exported as a 'highly potent ground attack combat fighter'.[14] It is thus ideally suited to conditions on East Timor.

According to the Indonesian human rights organisation, TAPOL, the aircraft has been seen at a military airbase on East Timor. Another of BAe's recent forays into the Indonesian market is the sale of five Battery Command Post Processors for improved field communications. This deal was announced in March 1987, just as the Indonesian armed forces were renewing their offensive against the resistance in East Timor. The British government claims that such weapons are not being used on East Timor but has made no effort to verify this. A further cause for concern is the large amount of training offered by the British Government to Indonesian military personnel: virtually every military unit in Indonesia has had combat experience in East Timor.

'Three aircraft bombed the Natarbora region, killing thousands of people. In particular, women, children and old people were killed, people who couldn't even run for cover. All we could do was pray for God's protection . . . The planes came in low and sprayed the ground with bullets, with their machine guns, killing many people.' – Christiano Costa, East Timorese refugee quoted in TAPOL Bulletin August 1988.

Falklands War – Bringing it all back home

The Falklands War between Britain and Argentina in April 1982 resulted in 1060 deaths. Some 770 British people and an even higher number of Argentinians were wounded. One of the most tragic aspects of this war was that British soldiers were killed by British-made weapons. Before the war, Britain was a major supplier of weapons to Argentina. British equipment exported included an aircraft carrier, two frigates, ship-to-air missiles, surface-to-air missiles, helicopters, bomber aircraft, sub-machine guns, radars and a wide range of support equipment. Components made by the British company, Plessey, were also present in the French Exocet missiles which were used extensively by Argentina.

'A girl friend who was writing to me while I was in the Falklands works for Plessey Connectors in Northampton. They have a contract with the company which makes Exocet missiles. In one of her letters she mentioned the massive amount of overtime she was suddenly being asked to do . . . The orders were being sent out to France . . . Just having the idea that someone I knew was making something which was being exported and used against me to kill me, just shows up the horrors of the arms trade.' – Falklands veteran, Wade Tidbury quoted in The Unnecessary War.

IRAN-IRAQ WAR – A CASE-STUDY

During the eighties, the Iran-Iraq war was the costliest in human lives and resources. At its outset in September 1980, most military experts predicted that the conflict would be very brief as it was thought that both sides would run out of armaments within a fortnight. Instead the fighting dragged on for eight years, partly because of the willingness of the world's arms-producing countries to supply the two sides with arms. In 1987, SIPRI identified twenty-six countries which had supplied arms to *both* warring parties. Britain was one such country. Although the British Government declared a ban on the sale of lethal military equipment to Iran and Iraq, in practice it is difficult to distinguish between lethal and non-lethal equipment. Even Colin Chandler, Head of the Defence Export Services Organisation (government arms trade promotion department) till 1988, admitted at a press conference in 1986 that 'there is no such thing as a non-lethal weapon'.[15] Throughout the conflict, so-called non-lethal equipment continued to flow to both sides.

British equipment legally exported to Iran during the Gulf War included:[16]

Spares for Chieftain and Scorpion tanks, air defence radar and three naval ships (one of which increased the Iranian navy's amphibious operations by one hundred per cent, according to an Iranian naval commander).

British equipment legally exported to Iraq during the Gulf War included:

Three hundred military Land Rovers and radar equipment. During the war, Iraq was also invited to British government arms fairs and Iraqi military personnel were trained by British armed forces in Britain.

War casualties

By the time of the UN ceasefire in August 1988, well over a million people [17] had been killed in a war which had resolved nothing. Unlike most other recent wars, much of the fighting took place on the borders of Iran and Iraq and the majority of casualties were military. The enormous number of deaths was partly a consequence of the First World War human wave tactics adopted by Iran to overcome the numerically smaller but better equipped Iraqi army. Poor peasant people from the rural areas of Iran provided the cannon fodder for these battles.

The cost to ordinary people

While most of the casualties were soldiers, civilians in Iran and Iraq did not escape the ravages of war. Hundreds were killed in the 'war of the cities' when the two sides sent long-distance missiles hurtling into each other's major cities. Thousands more remain homeless, having had their homes destroyed during the eight years of war or having fled their towns and villages to avoid the fighting. In Iran, for example, more than a million people displaced in the first months of the war are still living in makeshift homes on the fringes of Tehran.

(below) Iranian in the
ruins of his
house destroyed
by Iraqi bombers
(Kaveh Golestan/Network)

(above) Bodies of
Iraqi soldiers
(Kaveh Golestan/Network)

LETTER FROM IRAN

*'It takes the Iraqi bombers 7 minutes to reach Tehran from the
borders. It takes us almost as long to reach our mousehole in the
basement after the sirens blare . . . Suddenly we hear a boom, a
second, and then a third . . . One of the bombs missed us by only
800m. It exploded, turning a four-storey building into a heap of
rubble . . . Eighteen people are under that rubble. My wife's
relatives from the province of Bakhtaran have come to visit us.
"Visit" is perhaps not well chosen. For more than two months they
lived on the hills around the city and we had no news of them . . .
Finally I located them in the safety of a small cottage. They looked
haggard and utterly hopeless. I told them I had come to take them to
Tehran. But my brother-in-law would not listen. "I have to find out
what happened to my house!" I suggested that we go and take a
look. We drove into this wasteland of a city . . . "Stop here!" my
companion said. He got out and took off towards a mound of rubble.
"Is this the place?" I asked. He shook his head and sat down on the
heap. Suddenly he began to dig with his hands, scooping away
rocks, bricks and mud. I tried to lead him away. "Let's go! The
planes may come any minute!" But he was insane with despair.
"Fifty years of my life! Fifty years! Gone for good!" '* – Morad
Shukri in South May 1987

Shattered economies

Eight years ago, Iran and Iraq were amongst the richest states in the
Middle East with huge oil revenues and expanding economies. Today,
both countries are facing economic ruin, war having consumed 40% of
Iran's income and 60% of Iraq's.[18] All hope of a balanced development
independent of western companies and foreign banks has now been
destroyed. Iraq, for example, which had foreign reserves of $20 billion in
1979 is now one of the most heavily indebted nations in the world.
Neither country can even begin to reconstruct without further heavy
borrowing from abroad. The cost of the destruction of industrial plant,
cities and infrastructure in the war zone and from the missile attacks on
cities is estimated at up to $600 billion.[19] For ordinary people, prolonged
economic crisis spells further shortages, long queues, inflation and low
wages – difficulties they have already had to live with during the war
years.

'Meagre shows of lights and bunting are easily eclipsed by the lamp-lit kiosks at every corner . . . These are the only oases of colour in a city (Tehran) noted for its drabness, and made worse by constant electricity cuts, partial black-outs and a chronic shortage of heating oil, which leaves people pinched and cold as the winds sweep down from the snow-covered mountains which surround the Iranian capital.' – John Bulloch in The Independent 3.2.87.

Future wars?

A number of regional arms races are currently in progress in certain regions of the Third World where political tensions are particularly high. If British arms companies continue to sell such large amounts of weaponry to countries involved in these arms races, then fragile peace could well break down and open warfare develop.

Gulf Co-operation states

It has been argued that the Iran-Iraq war was partly the outcome of the massive rearmament programmes undertaken by Iraq and particularly by Iran during the 1970s. This followed the oil price rises of that period which swelled revenues for these two oil-producing governments. By 1975 Iran was the single largest purchaser of US arms in the world.

In the light of the bloodshed caused by the Iran-Iraq war, many now regard the massive rearmament programmes of the neighbouring Gulf states with some alarm. As with Iran and Iraq, arms sales to the oil-rich Gulf states (Bahrain, Kuwait, Oman, Qatar, Saudi Arabia) shot up in the 1970s as a result of oil price rises. They have been amassing huge stockpiles of weapons ever since, but particularly following the outbreak of the Iran-Iraq war. In 1981, these states (listed above) founded the Gulf Co-operation Council (GCC), one of the main purposes of which was to pool and expand the military capability of its members so as to deter attack from the Gulf War belligerents.

The GCC's formal support for Iraq and its lavish financial donations to the Iraqi war effort remind us that the attitude of the GCC states to the Gulf War was far from neutral. It is still possible that at some future point Iran might regard the massive armament programmes of its conservative Arab neighbours as a threat requiring a response. In addition there is the threat which this arms build-up poses to the cold war relations betwen Israel and the GCC states, none of which recognise the state of Israel. The scenario of war amongst the GCC states is particularly horrific when one considers the strategic and economic importance of the region to the superpowers and to the industrialised world as a whole, based on its vast oil reserves. The arrival of western naval ships in the Gulf during the final year of the Iran-Iraq war demonstrates the willingness of the major world powers to become involved in the region's conflicts.

Britain has actively and aggressively fuelled the arms race in the Gulf region and is a major supplier of weapons to the GCC states.[20] The most obvious example of this in recent years has been the huge sales of Tornado fighter aircraft to Saudi Arabia. The first deal signed in 1985 was worth £5 billion and doubled the value of the British arms trade overnight. But the second deal in 1988 broke all records, involving a sum of between £10 and £15 billion.

India and Pakistan

There is a history of conflict between these two countries which has culminated in three major wars since World War II. A long-standing border dispute continues and sporadic skirmishes have occurred. In 1987, SIPRI elevated this border conflict to the status of a full-scale war because of the escalating fatalities on the disputed Siachin glacier. To add to the tension, India suspects Pakistan of supplying Sikh extremists in the Punjab with weapons. Under the guise of 'military manoeuvres', the two armies lined their borders in the spring of 1987, coming close to open conflict.[21]

The implications of war between India and Pakistan are particularly serious, in view of the huge arsenals which both countries have amassed over the last two decades. In 1987 India was the world's largest buyer of arms,[22] accounting for one fifth of all Third World orders. Meanwhile Pakistan has ready access to the most advanced of US weapons. The two countries have been locked in a dangerous arms race, aggravated by both countries' suspected development of nuclear weapons. Rajiv Ghandi, Prime Minister of India, has been quoted as saying that his country would reconsider its non-nuclear military policy if it discovered that Pakistan had atomic weapons. Referring to India's growing military strength, the late President Zia said: 'We have to match sword with sword, tank with tank, and destroyer with destroyer.'[23] Although the election of Benazir Bhutto as Prime Minister of Pakistan in 1988 gave some hope for improved relations in the region, the armed forces remain a powerful force in Pakistan. Britain's arms trade has served to aggravate the Indo-Pakistani arms race.

Weapons recently sold to India include:
Harrier fighter aircraft; Jaguar fighter aircraft; Sea King helicopters; Sea Eagle air-to-ship missiles; Hermes aircraft carrier.

Weapons recently sold to Pakistan include:
1 destroyer; 2 frigates; targets for testing new ship-board weapon system. In April 1988 Lord Trefgarne, Minister for Defence Procurement, visited Pakistan to try and sell more frigates to the Pakistani Navy.

Military personnel from both countries receive training from British armed forces.

Conclusion

British weapons have fuelled a considerable number of wars and arms races in recent years. Almost without exception, these 'trouble spots' have been in the Third World and most of the casualties have been civilian. Although imported weapons are not the root cause of this conflict, they have served to raise tensions and prolong and escalate the fighting.

NOTES

1: Mrs Thatcher argued this case in a speech at the Lord Mayor's banquet, November 1986.
2: See Ruth Sivard: *World Military and Social Expenditures 1986* (WMSE) p. 27.
3: *SIPRI Yearbook 1988* – based on definition of war which is over 1000 war-related deaths.
4: See *South* August 1986.
5: See *WMSE 1987/88* p. 28.
6: Ibid.
7: Quoted in *New Internationalist*, March 1983.
8: Quoted in Michael T. Klare: 'The Arms Trade: Changing Patterns in the 1980s'.
9: *South* August 1986.
10: See *Daily Telegraph* 23.7.87.
11: In March 1987 CAAT received photographs taken by Lord Winchelsea of British field guns installed on King Hassan's desert wall.
12: See CAAT briefing, 'British arms sales to South Africa' and chapter 9 for further information.
13: See chapter 6 on Indonesia.
14: Quoted in an advertisement in *Flight International* 4.3.78.
15: Colin Chandler quoted at a press conference at the British Army Equipment Exhibition, June 1986.
16: 'Legally exported' equipment means equipment exported with the permission of the British Government.
17: This is based on estimates of western military analysts. Iraq has claimed that its forces killed around 800,000 Iranians. However, Iran now claims that it lost no more than 123,220 military personnel and 11,000 civilians.

18: Figures in *South*, September 1988.
19: Ibid.
20: See CAAT Briefing 'Oil, Arms and the GCC states' for full list of British arms sales to GCC states.
21: See *SIPRI Yearbook* 1988.
22: Information in this paragraph is from an article by John Kegan in the *Daily Telegraph* 19.8.88.
23: Quoted in *Jane's Defence Weekly* 16.7.88.

CHAPTER 10
Third World arms industry[1]

'One of the most noted, though least studied, changes in the Third World' is how one researcher has described Third World arms production.[2] Though comprising only 1.5 – 2% of global production,[3] it has undergone a massive expansion in recent years. Thirty years ago, the number of Third World arms producers was confined to no more than five: Argentina, Egypt, Colombia, India, and North Korea. In the late 1960s these were joined by Brazil, Israel, and South Africa and from then on more and more countries entered the ranks of the arms producers. By the 1980s around 40 countries[4] were producing and exporting weapons. The resulting value of Third World arms production in 1984 was estimated to be 500 times higher in real terms than what it had been in 1950.[5]

The *type* of weapons manufactured varies considerably but most common amongst Third World countries is the production of ammunition, a relatively simple process involving the assembly of just a few components. The second most common production venture is that of

Rank order of the main Third World major-weapon producing countries 1950–84 and 1980–84; shares in percentages.
Figures may not add up to totals due to rounding.

Source: *Arms Production in the Third World* – SIPRI – Ed. Michael Brozska and Thomas Ohlson (Taylor and Francis, 1986)

Rank/country	1950–84	Of which licensed production (per cent)	1980–84	Rank for 1980–84
1. India	3 923	77	1 265	(2)
2. Israel	2 885	4	1 342	(1)
3. South Africa	1 143	62	380	(6)
4. Brazil	1 116	26	566	(3)
5. Taiwan	1 051	85	562	(4)
6. Korea, North	775	41	265	(8)
7. Argentina	599	34	391	(5)
8. Korea, South	478	58	346	(7)
9. Egypt	289	57	162	(9)
10. ASEAN countries	249	84	109	(10)
Others	200		121	
Total	**12 707**	**50**	**5 509**	

THIRD WORLD ARMS INDUSTRY

Shares of selected countries in total Third World major-weapon production, 1950–64, 1965–79 and 1980–84. Countries are ranked according to their share for 1980–84.

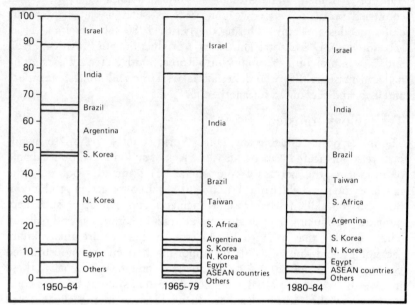

Value of production of major weapons in the Third World, 1950–84.

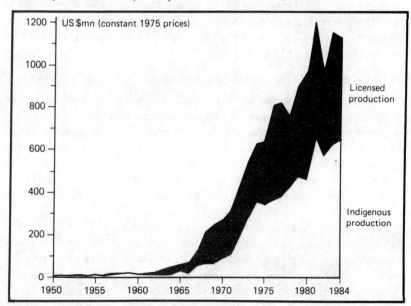

Source : *Arms Production in the Third World* – SIPRI – Ed. Brozska and Ohlson.

ships, followed by aircraft – usually less advanced aircraft, such as transports, trainers and lightplanes. Only a handful of Third World countries produce *major* weapon systems such as jet fighter aircraft, missiles and tanks. During the period 1980–84, Israel and India accounted for 47% of total Third World production. South Africa, Brazil and Taiwan took up 17% while North Korea, South Korea and Argentina had an 18% share. Egypt, Indonesia, Malaysia, the Philippines, Singapore and Thailand accounted for another 4%.[6]

Technology transfer

The major obstacle facing any Third World country wishing to manufacture sophisticated armaments is the lack of an industrial base capable of producing the necessary components. This includes not only the machine tools and electronic equipment required for actual production, but also the skilled workers and engineers and a host of subsidiary industries producing high quality metals, radios, computers and plastics. The only way that a Third World country can acquire this military technology and know-how is by importing it from the industrialised countries via licensing and co-production agreements. Usually, these involve the whole or partial assembly of weapon systems by arms companies from the industrialised world on location in the client Third World countries. The sale of licences to Third World countries for the manufacture of major weapons is dominated by a handful of countries – the US, Britain, France, West Germany, and the USSR. Together, these countries account for 85% of all licences.[7] Most licences are for the production of ships (35%) and aircraft (43%).[8]

What's in it for the supplier countries

The industrialised countries have sometimes been reluctant to export their technologies for fear of creating competitors or of passing on sensitive military know-how which could find its way to enemy powers. The US, for example, has enforced strict regulations to control the export of its technology and only allows manufacture under licence in some nine countries, despite being the world's largest arms trader. Similarly, Soviet designs have only been produced in India and North Korea.

Western European countries such as Britain, on the other hand, have been relatively lax on this issue and have actively promoted technology transfer, not through any desire to nurture Third World military independence but for pragmatic commercial reasons. Firstly, the equipment which a Third World country needs to acquire before building up an arms industry may be far more expensive than the finished article itself.

Naval vessels can be produced more cheaply in the Third World. *(Fairey Marine)*

That means more contracts (at least for an initial period) and thus more profits for foreign licensers. The costs of producing F-5 fighter aircraft under licence in South Korea and Taiwan, for example, proved much higher than the production costs in the US.[9] In one particular case, the cost of producing a communications device in South Africa was nine times the cost of a similar device produced in Europe or the US.[10]

While it usually costs more to produce in the Third World, certain types of weapons can be made more cheaply than in the industrialised world, mainly because wages are lower. The construction of naval vessels, for example, a labour-intensive exercise, usually costs less in the Third World. Keeping costs down can be attractive to licensing companies, as it enables them to undercut competitors. At a time when debt-ridden countries are finding it difficult to pay for major weapons systems, arms companies have much to gain from reducing their prices.

Another advantage of producing weapons under licence in the Third World is often the more relaxed state control, taking the form of lower taxation or less stringent export regulations.

Singapore – a haven for multinationals

Cheap labour costs and 'advantageous commercial regulations' (including lax export regulations) are cited by SIPRI as the two major motivations behind the activities of multinational arms companies in Singapore.[11] A variety of weapons is being produced under licence

Singapore docks *(Jenny Matthews/Format)*

there for export, often through the establishment of local subsidiary companies. One of Singapore's largest shipyards, for example, belongs to a subsidiary of the British company, Vosper Thorneycroft. United Scientific Holdings (UK) produces military optical devices through its subsidiary, Avimo Singapore while Racal/Decca (UK) is currently producing electronic equipment under licence with the Government-owned Singapore Technology Corporation (STC). In 1986 plans were afoot to form a subsidiary of Racal in Singapore. It is through the collaboration of these big foreign companies (many of them British) that Singapore now has a sizeable arms export trade. This includes sales to controversial countries in the Middle East and to several Latin American countries to whom the licensing European companies might not normally be able to sell directly, owing to their own governments' more stringent restrictions. The Swedish company, Bofors, forbidden by Swedish law from trading with countries at war and human rights violators, managed to sell surface-to-air missiles to Iran during the Gulf war by transporting them via Singapore. Similarly some forty Bofors naval guns delivered to Singapore between 1979 and 1985 were re-exported to Thailand, Taiwan, and South Korea.

Turkey – cheap labour

In Turkey, too, cheap labour is being offered as an incentive for foreign arms companies to set up production. Turkish Prime Minister Ozal has been quoted as saying: 'workers in Turkey are low paid . . . arms manufacturers ought to set up armaments industry jointly with big private holdings in Turkey'.[12] Having banned trade unions, the government clearly intends to guarantee these low wages. Plans are afoot to invest $20 billion of state funds over the next few years in the manufacture of equipment ranging from armoured vehicles to military aircraft. Several British companies are now taking advantage of these conditions. In 1986, a Turkish government publication reported talks on joint production deals with GEC-Marconi (for Tigerfish torpedoes), Royal Ordnance (for Chieftain tanks), and GKN (for Warrior armoured personnel carriers). Vickers is also thought to have signed a licensed agreement for tank production. Meanwhile Marconi recently announced the formation of an electronics company to be based near Ankara.

Technology transfer in a buyers' market

It would appear then, that licence and co-production deals often have lucrative spin-offs for the arms companies of the industrialised world. Yet at a time when arms sales worldwide are falling, it is the buyers and not the sellers who set the agenda. Most of the pressure for technology transfers is now coming from Third World governments themselves. Increasingly, they are saying to the foreign arms companies: 'We'll buy your weapons only if you let us build a good proportion of them and if you help us build up our own arms industry.' In this climate, arms companies are having to attract Third World clients with promises of technology transfer deals.

Self-sufficiency – a facade

Arms production is often portrayed as a step in the direction of self-sufficiency and independence for Third World countries. Few states like being in a position where their military defence is dependent on a handful of foreign suppliers. Significantly, almost all of the major Third World arms producers – Taiwan, South Africa, Israel, Brazil, Argentina and Chile, to name a few – established arms industries in response to arms supply problems or embargoes imposed against them.

Yet in reality this self-sufficiency is a facade. Third World arms industries have only been sustained through the co-operation and active involvement of the arms-producing countries of the industrialised world. Even countries isolated by embargoes such as South Africa could never have formed their own arms industries, had there not been loopholes in the arms embargoes, enabling them to continue importing military technology and equipment from abroad.

South Africa – evading the embargo

Despite the existence of an extensive industrial base, the apartheid regime continues to rely on imports from Western countries in certain crucial areas – particularly electronics and aircraft components. According to evidence presented to the UN Security Council arms embargo committee, over half of South Africa's arms procurement budget in 1984 was spent on arms purchases from abroad. It has been estimated that around 90% of South Africa's arms manufacture is based on foreign industry, and much of this emanates from Britain. South Africa's new Oliphant tank, for example, is merely a modernised version of the British Centurion tank.

South Africa has been able to acquire foreign military technology because of the many loopholes in the UN embargo on arms sales to the apartheid regime. One such loophole is the trade in dual use equipment – items which have a civilian as well as a military application. According to the British Government's interpretation, only equipment 'specifically designed for military use' is prohibited. Because of this narrow definition of the embargo, a number of British companies continue to be involved in the South African arms industry. In 1984, for example, it was reported that Plessey was responsible for the commercial development and manufacture of the Tellurometer, an electronic distance measuring device, from which a military model has been designed for range findings.[13]

South African Alpha XH-1 helicopter

Drawbacks to licensed production

The hope of Third World governments is that through co-production and licensing agreements, they will eventually be able to produce their own indigenous weapon models, using the technology and expertise established by the foreign companies. Yet in practice licensing and co-production schemes rarely enable Third World countries to become self-sufficient in arms production. The only countries which have been able to follow up licensed production with indigenous designs are Israel and Brazil. A number of countries have gone on to copy hull designs from licence-built warships for their own domestically designed ships but have still had to import various components.

As long as a country's general economic and social progress lags behind advances in military technology, it will be unable to acquire the technical skills required to replace the foreign licenser. Moreover with less advanced arms production facilities, there are often lengthy gaps between, say, design and start of production, or between production and deployment. When the military item is eventually produced, it may well have fallen out of date. Officials at Northrop Aircraft estimate that by the time a foreign producer has taken over full production of a US-designed weapon, it will be six to ten years old, by which time it would have long since been overtaken by new models developed much more quickly in the US or Europe for Third World customers.[14] Industrialised nations will therefore continue to hold a monopoly over the latest military technology.

Economic disaster

Whatever the level of dependence on foreign arms companies, arms production nearly always imposes great strains on a Third World economy. The new military complex absorbs scarce government revenue and skilled workers. Such expenditure is like pouring money down a drain because, once made, arms can only be used for destruction. They create relatively few jobs and very little consumer spending, thus adding nothing to the civilian economy. Heavy investment in arms production also has the effect of pushing civilian industry towards high level technology. This may be totally inappropriate both to the advancement of a semi-industrialised economy and to the pressing needs of a poverty-ridden population. On top of this, arms production has worrying social consequences. Although wages throughout the Third World are low compared to those in the industrialised world, skilled Third World workers still earn more than the average local rate. Since military industries draw on the highly skilled few rather than the unskilled masses, they serve to widen the gap between rich and poor. Higher wages in turn stimulate a standard of living way out of line with that of the general populace, creating little islands of wealth amidst a sea of poverty. Therefore the argument that arms production enhances the economic and social development of Third World countries holds little water.

WORKING CONDITIONS

Conditions for workers in many Third World arms factories are poor, as revealed by an accident which took place in Chile. A factory owned by the Chilean arms company, Cardoen, was operating a twelve-hour shift on an assembly-line involved in highly delicate weapon manufacture. In 1986, workers assembling a 500lb bomb to be exported to Iraq accidently set off a series of explosions which ripped through the factory, killing over fifty people. Local inhabitants claimed that appalling working conditions and long shifts were the cause of these explosions.[15]

A Brazilian trade union journal reported in 1987 that there had been several fatal accidents in the town of Piquete caused by explosions in local arms factories.[16]

A CRITIQUE OF THE BRAZILIAN ARMS INDUSTRY

The following extract is taken from the magazine of the Brazilian Metalworkers' Union representing arms workers in Sao Jose dos Campos, where 80% of Brazil's military production takes place.

'Although it is true to say that the Brazilian arms industry has attained a certain degree of autonomy, it is heavily dependent on imported components. CACEX's (Foreign Trade Department, Bank of Brazil) method of presenting data makes it difficult to tell what components are being imported. But we know that the main bottlenecks in the Brazilian economy are in fields such as precision mechanics, microelectronics and computer technology, fields which demand a level of technical know-how that Brazil does not have. So this much-lauded autonomy is a long way from being achieved. It is just used as an argument to justify continued government expenditure on the industry.

The amount of public money used to guarantee the current level of arms exports is very high. The tax exemptions granted to the industry mean that the government is effectively handing over to these companies money that could be spent on health, education, public transport etc. The government and therefore all taxpayers are, in effect, financing the arms industry. This money is never officially counted as military expenditure. If the money invested in the arms industry were invested in other sectors of the economy, it would generate hard currency from exports in just the same way. Alternatively it could be used to satisfy the basic needs of the population. This might not help to pay the foreign debt but at least it would mean that the Brazilian people could live with a little more dignity.

It would be rash to talk about the Brazilian arms industry having a brilliant future. The level of international demand has been falling and competition is increasing.' – *Apoio Sindical* March 1988 – Magazine of the Metalworkers' Union of Sao Jose dos Campos.

Brazilian slums. Arms production does not benefit the Brazilian poor.
(Jenny Matthews/ Format)

The real motives behind arms production

If arms production does not lessen the dependency of Third World countries on the arms-producing countries of the industrialised world and does not contribute to economic growth, one may wonder why Third World governments are so keen to establish indigenous arms industries. The motives appear to be mainly political. Domestic arms production is regarded as holding more status than the import of weapons from another country. Even where an arms industry is far from being able to supply its armed forces comprehensively, self-sufficiency is often claimed, as can be seen from government reports in Egypt, India, Chile, and Israel. Nationalism is an important ingredient in legitimising political power and governments are boosted by claims of military self-sufficiency. Therefore an arms industry – however dependent on foreign arms companies – plays an important propaganda role in many Third World countries.

Role of the military

The Third World countries which have made the greatest strides towards establishing their own arms industries are often those dominated by military or authoritarian regimes. Soldiers as rulers tend to be strongly in favour of arms production not just for reasons of prestige, but also because it can be used as a tool for the armed forces to make their imprint on the economy and can provide jobs and income for retired military personnel. In Israel, a country with a powerful army commanding extensive influence over the civilian government, most officers eventually pass through a revolving door from staff positions in the armed forces to executive roles in arms companies. Such a 'retirement' is regarded as a reward for the active battlefield service which most Israeli officers have undertaken over the many years Israel has been at war. This may explain why there are as many as 700 military firms in a country with a population of only four million.

Third World arms exporters

Many Third World arms producers are now expanding their arms industries, not so as to increase supplies to their own armed forces but in order to *export* their wares. At least half of the Third World arms producers are now involved in the arms trade and in some cases arms exports have become a centrepiece of entire economies. In Israel, for example, military exports represent 25% of *all* Israeli exports (compared to 1% of visible exports in Britain). The justification normally provided by the governments concerned is that arms exports generate foreign exchange

THIRD WORLD ARMS INDUSTRY

Rank order of main Third World major-weapon exporters, 1950–84.
Figures are in US$million, at constant (1975) prices; shares in percentages.
Figures may not add up to totals due to rounding.
(Excludes re-exports of imported weapons).

Source: *Arms Production in the Third World* – SIPRI – Ed. Brozska and Ohlson.

Rank/country	1950–84	Of which exported during 1980–84 (per cent)
1. Brazil	629	72
2. Israel	595	58
3. Korea, South	173	79
4. South Africa	54	91
5. Indonesia	34	94
6. Singapore	32	13
7. Egypt	20	85
8. Argentina	17	94
9. India	10	80
10. Korea, North	6	50
Others	2	
Total	**1 571**	

Value of exports of major conventional weapons from Third World countries, 1970–84.

Source: *Arms Production in the Third World* – SIPRI – Ed. Brozska and Ohlson

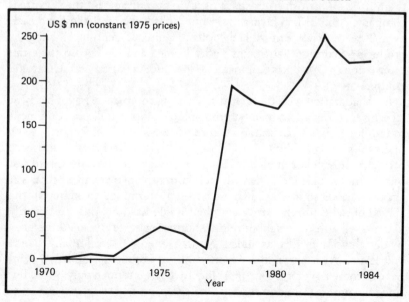

(ie. dollars) of which there is a great shortage in most Third World countries. Yet in reality military exports rarely benefit the economies which have produced them. Israel's foreign debt, for example, has risen to $30 billion, despite its burgeoning arms trade. Brazil, another leading Third World arms exporter, remains deep in economic crisis with a debt of $116 billion. Generally the money made on arms sales simply goes towards paying the interest on foreign debts (many of them accumulated through military purchases) or is recycled by the military complex for the purchase of yet more military equipment.

It is easy to condemn some Third World arms trading countries both for their short-sighted economic planning and also for their lax controls on arms exports. Yet we must not lose sight of the fact that to a large extent the Third World arms trade is a creation of the industrialised countries of the North, as has been explained above. It is only with their active and willing collaboration that Third World arms producers have been able to start exporting, as the following case-study reveals.

Egyptian arms exports – a case-study of British involvement

Although Egyptian ministers pride themselves on having established an indigenous and independent 'arsenal for the Middle East', in reality their arms industry is heavily dependent on foreign arms companies, many of them British. British Aerospace is a joint partner in the Egyptian company, Arab British Dynamics, while Rolls Royce and Westland each own 30% of Arab British Helicopters. United Scientific Holdings is producing Scorpion light tanks under licence and has set up the Arab International Optronics company to produce a variety of electronic equipment.

In collaboration with these British licensing companies, Egypt has kept its arms factories afloat mainly through huge sales of military equipment to Iraq for its war against Iran. According to Middle East Report,[17] 70% of Egypt's arms exports in 1987 went to Iraq. The British Aerospace Swingfire missile assembled in Egypt is thought to have been sold not only to Iraq but also to Sudan which is currently involved in a brutal war against various southern Sudanese tribes. Determined to stonewall the spread of radicalism in Africa and the Middle East, Egypt is particularly keen to sell arms to neighbouring authoritarian governments threatened by destabilisation, such as Sudan, North Yemen, Oman, Jordan, Nigeria and Zaire. With an annual export value of around $2 billion,[18] arms have become Egypt's second most lucrative item, topped only by oil. But since the profits from arms exports are either used to service debts or are ploughed back into the Egyptian Ministry of Defence to purchase more arms from the West, they are of little benefit to the Egyptian economy.

Nuclear and missile proliferation

The transfer of military technology from the industrialised world to the Third World is also encouraging an expansion of the global nuclear 'club'. Using the military technology originally imported via foreign arms companies, many Third World arms producers such as Israel, South Africa, Argentina, Brazil, Pakistan, and India are now developing their own nuclear weapons. According to the School of Peace Studies at Bradford University, thirteen more countries may have nuclear arsenals by the turn of the century. Meanwhile, many of the leading Third World arms producers are developing powerful, long-range missiles – once again with the help of the arms industries of the North. Some of these missiles can carry warheads of 500 kilograms over a distance of 300 kilometers. Possession of such weapons enormously increases a country's military capacity. Israel's Jericho II missile can hit targets as far away as Egypt and Argentina will be able to reach the Falklands/Malvinas Islands from the Argentinian mainland. The alarming spread of missile technology was described by the usually sober *Financial Times* as a 'deadly race out of control.'[19] Such missiles could be equipped relatively easily with nuclear and chemical warheads and most of the countries involved in this long-range missile proliferation are also those suspected of having nuclear and chemical weapon capabilities.

Conclusion

The benefits of arms production to Third World countries are questionable. In most cases, this type of production does little to improve internal economic conditions or to lessen dependency on foreign arms companies. All Third World arms industries remain tied to the transfer of technology from leading arms-producing countries like Britain. Technology transfer may be a less visible sign of the global arms race than the straightforward export of finished weapons systems but its implications are equally dangerous. On one level, it has led to a widening of the arms export market as the more advanced of the Third World arms producers start to trade their wares. This has further restricted the prospects for controlling the arms trade. On another level, the trade in technology has enabled more and more countries to develop advanced weapons – including nuclear weapons and long-range missiles, thereby narrowing the possibilities for lasting global peace.

NOTES

1: China is excluded from the category of Third World arms producers because of the complexities, magnitude and long history of arms production in that country.
2: Michael Brzoska: 'The impact of arms production in the Third World'. Occasional Paper published by Center for International Studies, University of Missouri-St Louis, March 1987, p. 1.
3: See SIPRI: *Arms production in the Third World* ed. Michael Brzoska and Thomas Ohlson (Taylor and Francis, London and Philadelphia 1986), p. 7.
4: *Jane's Yearbook.*
5: See SIPRI: *Arms production in the Third World* p. 7.
6: Op. cit. p. 10.
7: Op. cit. p. 25.
8: Op. cit. p. 26.
9: See Michael Brozska, p. 16.
10: See South African Ministry of Defence, White Paper 1977, supplement to Paratus, May 1977.
11: See SIPRI: *Arms production in the Third World* p. 72.
12: Quoted in *Dayanisma*, January 1989 (Turkish newsletter produced in Britain).
13: See *The Guardian* 18.4.84.
14: See *Bombs for Breakfast* (COPAT 1981) p. 40.
15: See *The Guardian* 27.1.86.
16: Reported in *Apoio Sindical* No. 1, March 1988, Sao Jose dos Campos, Brazil.
17: See Joe Stark: 'Arms Industries of the Middle East' in *Middle East Report* (MERIP) January 1987, p. 13.
18: See *International Herald Tribune* 15.6.85.
19: See *Financial Times* 8.6.88.

CHAPTER 11
Prospects for change

The arms trade to the Third World has brought violence, poverty and destruction in its path. Yet, despite the gloomy picture we have painted, there is some hope for limiting and eventually ending this trade. Great efforts have already been made, both in the supplier countries of the North and in the recipient countries of the South. Ordinary people worldwide have mounted campaigns and many governments have also taken measures to control the arms trade.

Grassroots initiatives

European campaigns

Across Europe there are now organisations working to end the arms trade in Austria, Belgium, Britain, Denmark, France, Italy, the Netherlands, Spain, Sweden, Switzerland, and West Germany. With the growing incidence of collaboration between European arms companies

French anti-arms trade campaign, COVA, pickets an arms company, February 1989 in protest against Chile's arrest of a journalist who wrote a critical article about a French deal with the Chilean navy.

and the increasing importance of Europe as a single political entity, a network of European organisations campaigning against the arms trade was formed in 1984. Regular meetings of the Network are held every six months to exchange information and experiences. In 1988 the Network campaigned around a report on the arms trade submitted to the European Parliament by the British MEP, Glyn Ford. Also in 1988, BUKO of West Germany and Campaign Against Arms Trade of the UK co-operated with the World Campaign Against Military Collaboration with Apartheid to stop the sale of multi-sensor platforms (missile tracking devices) from West Germany to South Africa. This campaign achieved its objective.

Britain: Campaign Against Arms Trade was set up in 1974 by a number of peace organisations who were concerned about the growth of the arms trade following the Middle East war of 1973 and the rise in oil prices.[1] In the long-term, CAAT's aim is to end all arms trade. In the meantime, the Campaign has focussed on trying to persuade the British Government and major political parties to increase controls on the arms trade, reduce the secrecy surrounding the British arms trade, and put an end to government promotion of the arms trade. Major campaigns have been launched against the two Government-sponsored arms fairs – the British Army Equipment Exhibition and the Royal Navy Equipment Exhibition – held in alternate years. CAAT has also protested against sales of British weapons to human rights violators such as the regimes of Pinochet in Chile and Suharto in Indonesia, and to countries at war (particularly Iran and Iraq during the Gulf War). As a means of safeguarding the jobs which would be lost if the British arms trade were to be stopped, CAAT has pressed for the conversion of military industry to civilian production.

Campaigns in the Third World

Although most anti-arms trade work has been undertaken in the supplier countries, a number of campaigns against the arms trade and related issues have also been launched in some recipient Third World countries.

Thailand: March 17 1987 was the first day of the Defense Asia '87 arms exhibition in Bangkok. As the exhibition opened, around 60 protesters of the Thai Coalition for Peace and Development gathered near the entrance. The large banner which led their procession read, 'Defence through development not armament'. A simple drama was acted on the footpath near the entrance to this 'market of death' involving a giant set of scales with bombs on one side and medicine and vegetables on the other.[2]

Campaign Against Arms Trade torchlit vigil outside the DESO, December 1987
(Ivan Kyncl)

In December 1988, the Coalition for Peace and Development organised another demonstration against Defence Asia '88. The co-ordinator of this demonstration, Laddawan Tantivitayapitak wrote:

'This year, at the press conference set up by the exhibition organisers, we submitted a petition to the spokesman of the Thai armed forces, Lt Gen. Naruedol Dejpradiyuth. The arms exhibition in no way benefits our people, the majority of whom are poor. We asked the government and the army to withdraw its support for the arms exhibition. When we were submitting our petition, I had a long argument with the Lt Gen. who finally refused to accept the petition. However, our argument was well publicised in almost every newspaper in Bangkok. A month before the exhibition day, we organised a drawing contest for students in Bangkok and up country. 150 pictures showing the danger of arms were sent in. On the opening day of the exhibition, we organised children to march by with some of the drawings. Nevertheless, it was announced at the exhibition press conference that another arms exhibition will be held in March 1989. This is a warning to us to work harder.'[3]

India: In July 1985 the people of Baliepal and Bhograi in Orissa province, eastern India learned that 400 sq. km of their land was earmarked for a missile testing range. Apparently the Indian Ministry of Defence want to use the land to develop long-range missiles, largely based on designs of

Thai Coalition for Peace and Development demonstrates at the Defense Asia Exhibition, December 1988.

imported Soviet missiles. Villagers were told they would have to vacate their traditional farming land.

Popular opposition to the missile range began with the launching of a petition. Following the government's issue of eviction orders to 110,000 people, volunteer squads were formed which successfully and non-violently prevented government officials and police from entering the area. At the time of writing (1988), vigils were being held in all 126 villages of Orissa. When unidentified persons were spotted, conch shells were blown and villagers converged on the spot. Civil liberties groups were supporting the villagers, and demonstrations were held throughout the province. The Government's response was to impose an economic blockade. Supplies of sugar, kerosene and wheat were not allowed into the area while local cash crops on which many local farmers are dependent for income, were not allowed out. Local students have been denied documents necessary to compete for scholarships.

Brazil: As the slump in the global arms trade deepens, redundancies and wage cuts are becoming commonplace in the Brazilian arms industry, particularly since the Gulf War ceasefire (Iran and Iraq were major customers of Brazilian arms). This has provoked widespread discussion inside the Metalworkers' Union of Sao Jose dos Campos, one of the major unions representing arms workers, about the value of arms production and the possibilities for conversion of the Brazilian arms industry to civilian production. The union is also discussing conversion with trade unions in France and Italy. Articles in the union magazine, *Apoio Sindical*, have highlighted the many negative aspects of the Brazilian arms industry.

The President of the Sao Jose Metalworkers' Union explains the current strategy of his union:

'Our priority is to get a sound understanding of the arms industry. We want to make the workers here aware of what industry they are engaged in, of the products they help to make. We don't want them to just ignore this. When workers have no control over production, they have no interest in the finished product. It's a routine – you go to work and at the end of the shift you come home. All that matters is the money that comes in at the end of the month. But we are trying to think beyond that. We want to make workers aware that they too should begin to think about what they are producing, and think about who the company is selling these arms to.'[4]

Maurilio de Oliveira, a member of the Metalworkers' Union executive comments:

'In addition to being a threat to human lives, the arms industry is not economically viable. This is what we are trying to bring home to the workers.'[5]

Government attempts at arms trade limitation

History

The first multilateral attempt at controlling the arms trade to the Third World was made in 1890 when the colonial powers reached an agreement on regulating the export of arms to their respective African colonies. The details of this agreement, known as the Brussels Act, were mentioned in chapter 2 of our study. Far from reflecting any moral concerns on the part of the colonial powers, the Act was merely intended to prevent armed uprisings by native populations and to maintain the status quo of colonialism in Africa. It was only partially successful as nothing was done to control the extensive smuggling carried out by private arms merchants.

Moral arguments against the arms trade only started to be articulated during and after the First World War when outrage at the activities of private arms merchants prompted a flurry of multilateral arms transfer control proposals. Unilateral measures against countries at war [6] were also taken by some arms-producing countries, namely France, Spain and the US. However, the whole subject of controlling the arms trade disappeared altogether from the international agenda in the rising tide of international tension and rearmament preceding the Second World War.

After World War II, the international scene was dominated by US and Soviet efforts to expand their influence. Superpower bids for global hegemony also coloured the arms transfer controls of this period. For example, the Tripartite Declaration on the Middle East signed by Britain, France and the US in 1950 was largely intended as a tool to keep Middle Eastern countries firmly allied to the West. The Declaration specified that arms would only be sold if the recipient country agreed not to attack any other country in the region. So long as the western countries remained the sole suppliers of equipment to the Middle East, arms transfers could be effectively limited. However, all control efforts were eradicated and indeed reversed, when the western arms monopoly was broken by Egypt's order for weapons from Czechoslavakia and the USSR in 1955–56. Western countries were then eager to arm Egypt's neighbours regardless of their intentions, so as to counter eastern bloc influence.

In the sixties and seventies, there were sporadic attempts to block sales to individual countries at war. In 1963, for example, the UN Security Council imposed a partial arms embargo against Portugal when it refused to grant independence to its African territories. During the Nigerian Civil War 1967–70, public pressure forced a number of western governments, namely Italy, Belgium, the Netherlands and the US, to suspend all arms sales to the Nigerian government. Similarly, Israel's invasion of the West Bank of the River Jordan and the Gaza Strip in 1967 prompted several arms suppliers, including France, Israel's major supplier, to enforce an arms embargo against Israel. In 1977 the UN imposed a mandatory arms embargo on the apartheid regime of South Africa which is still adhered to today in varying degrees by a large number of arms-producing countries.

Carter's arms restraint policy

During this latter period the Third World policies pursued by the Kennedy and Carter administrations in the US – at least on the level of declared policy – contained some promise for controlling the arms trade. These two presidents argued that improved social and economic conditions rather than military heavyweight were the best guarantees against Soviet expansion in the Third World. The Carter arms export policy stated that the unrestrained spread of conventional weapons threatened stability in every region of the world and that the United

States – as the largest supplier – bore a special responsibility for slowing down the arms trade. To this end, Carter restricted arms supplies to the Middle East and to a number of governments who were renowned for their human rights violations, particularly in Latin America.

However by March 1980 Carter had effectively abandoned his arms restraint policy. The restrictions had only ever been implemented with the proviso that they could be waived in 'extraordinary circumstances' or when 'countries friendly to the United States must depend on advanced weaponry to offset qualitative and other disadvantages in order to maintain a regional balance.'[7] The fall of the Shah of Iran and the consequent 'need' to rearm Iran's pro-western neighbours as well as growing turmoil in Central America and Africa provided the Carter Administration with just the excuse for throwing arms trade control to the wind. In the final analysis, the arms trade researcher Michael T. Klare claims, President Carter never seriously challenged the belief that arms transfers served as a tool for the advancement of US foreign policy objectives.[8]

Arms trade control in the eighties

With the exception of the UN arms embargo on South Africa, no international treaty or other formal inter-state arrangement aimed at reducing the level of conventional arms transfers to the Third World is currently in force. Nevertheless a number of informal arms trade control agreements have been made over recent years. In 1982, the European Community leaders recommended that EC member countries impose an embargo against Israel following Israel's invasion of southern Lebanon. In 1989, amidst allegations that West German companies had helped build a chemical weapons plant in Libya, the EC member states approved export controls on eight key chemicals which could be used to make weapons. Outside the European Community, summit meetings of the western industrialised countries have occasionally urged each other to impose embargoes against countries accused of promoting terrorism such as Libya and Syria. However, with all these more informal arrangements, it has been left to the individual countries to decide whether or not to adopt any restraint. None could be described as internationally recognised embargoes.

European Parliament

Under the Treaty of Rome of 1957, the European Community has no jurisdiction over the military and security interests of its member states. Yet this has not stopped EC bodies such as the European Parliament from discussing the matter of arms exports. In 1983, a British Member of the European Parliament (MEP), Adam Fergusson, produced a report

119

which called on the Community to establish rules governing exports to non-Community countries and to agree on restrictions on certain types of arms to certain countries. At the time of writing (1988–89), another British MEP, Glyn Ford was presenting a report to the European Parliament on European arms exports which calls on the Community to remove some of the secrecy surrounding the arms trade, tighten customs and end-user procedures, assist industry wishing to move from military to civil production, and develop a common arms sales strategy. Both the Fergusson and Glyn Ford reports have been adopted by the European Parliament, although it remains to be seen whether they will alter the final policies of the Community.

Missile control

In response to the alarming proliferation of long-range missile technology,[9] a Missile Technology Control Regime (MTCR) was drawn up at a summit in April 1987 by the leading economic powers – the USA, Britain, France, West Germany, Italy, Canada, and Japan. The seven governments formulated common guidelines 'to control the transfer of equipment and technology which could make a contribution to any missile system capable of delivering a nuclear weapon.' This covers missiles which could carry a warhead of more than 500kg (1,100 lbs) and which could travel further than 300km (170 miles).

Although the MTCR is to be welcomed, it is only an agreement and not a treaty. It therefore has no status in international law. Moreover there is no machinery for monitoring or enforcing compliance to what is an entirely voluntary agreement. Most importantly, many of the biggest exporters of missiles and missile technology, such as China, the Soviet Union, North Korea and Argentina are not party to the agreement. The main possessors of missile technology – Egypt, Israel, Iraq, Saudi Arabia and Israel – are not involved either. Finally, the MTCR itself does not ban the export of missiles or missile technology but merely aims to 'restrain' such transfers.

CoCom agreement

The Co-ordinating Committee (CoCom) agreement is the only multilateral arms trade agreement which can claim to have been almost totally successful. This informal and secret agreement was initiated by the US in 1949 with the aim of preventing 'strategic materials' in the West from reaching Soviet bloc countries and Soviet allies. Although several countries have incorported the CoCom agreement into their own national export law, it has no standing in international law and officially does not exist. However CoCom membership is known to extend to all NATO countries excluding Iceland but including Japan. Several neutral countries like Sweden and Switzerland also appear to abide by the agreement. Any reluctant European states were brought into line in the post-war period by US threats to withhold funds for reconstruction. It is significant that several items regarded by the CoCom agreement as 'strategic' (and therefore not transferrable to Soviet bloc countries) are freely exported to South Africa by a number of NATO countries including Britain. This reflects the seriousness with which the CoCom agreement is implemented compared to the UN embargo against South Africa. Indeed, the success of the CoCom agreement demonstrates that international embargoes *can* work when the political will exists to enforce them.

Individual countries' controls

It was emphasised in chapter 1 that government policies of a number of individual arms-trading countries are becoming less stringent, as competition amongst the arms traders intensifies. Nevertheless, some arms-producing countries, namely Sweden, Norway, West Germany, the Netherlands, Denmark, and Canada, do have laws forbidding the export of arms to countries engaged in armed conflict and/or to countries whose governments have used military force to repress their people. These laws are enforced with varying degrees of success. Their effectiveness is often marred by gaping loopholes and by the atmosphere of secrecy which surrounds the arms trade, making it very difficult for neutral bodies to monitor governments' implementation of such laws.

British arms trade controls

Under the Export of Goods (Control) Order, British arms cannot be exported without a Government export licence. However, the Government does not publish any details of the criteria used to decide whether or not a licence should be granted. For example, unlike several other western countries, there is no British law against arms exports to countries engaged in war or to governments renowned for the violent repression of their people. Attempts to monitor the Government's arms trade policy have been thwarted by the thick wall of secrecy which surrounds the international arms trade. The Government is not obliged to release details of British arms sales and questions raised, either by members of the public or by MPs, are not answered.

At present, the British government only recognises two embargoes: the European Community embargo against Israel and the UN embargo against South Africa, the latter having been only partially successful because of Britain's narrow interpretation of this embargo.[10] In 1973, all British arms sales to Chile were halted in protest at the military coup against the Allende government. Yet, despite the continuing human rights violations of the Pinochet military regime, arms sales to Chile were resumed by the Thatcher Government in 1980.[11] Since then the Government has enforced embargoes against certain individual countries, but usually for short-term political reasons or in response to aggressive acts against Britain. For example, Britain imposed an embargo against Israel in 1982 mainly in order to placate Arab customers of British weapons who are anti-Israeli. An arms embargo was only imposed against Libya after a British policewoman was killed by a Libyan gunman outside the Libyan embassy in London. Similarly, stringent sanctions were enforced against Syria in 1986, because it was thought that the Syrian government had been involved in the Hindawi bomb plot to blow up an Israeli airliner departing from Heathrow. The escalating militarisation of the Middle East was not the issue in these cases.

However, at the international level, Britain has recently taken a more constructive approach to arms trade control. In his speech to the United Nations Third Special Session on Disarmament in June 1988, Foreign Secretary, Sir Geoffrey Howe questioned 'whether anyone benefits from remorselessly raising the ante in an endless game of military poker' and stressed that 'disarmanent is *not* just for NATO and the Warsaw pact. It is for *all* of us.' The British Government went on to call for 'greater openness on all types of international transfer of conventional weapons, including the possibility of establishing a United Nations register of arms transfers on a universal and non-discriminatory basis.' This fell far short of proposals put forward by Campaign Against Arms Trade as the register envisaged by the Government would only have listed annual monetary values of military production and imports and exports. However, Britain did at least help to gain international recognition of the need for more publicly available information on arms transfers.

Recipients' initiatives

Up until the 1970s all the arms trade limitation agreements had been initiated by the arms-producing *supplier* countries without any consultation with the recipient governments in the Third World. This was one of the reasons for the failure of many of these initiatives. It is true to say that arms control has had a very low priority for nearly all Third World governments. Yet to some extent this negative attitude derives from an inequality inherent in most of the proposals to limit the arms trade. While many Third World governments may place no more emphasis on military defence than governments in the industrialised countries, there is a crucial difference in attitudes to controlling the arms trade. 'The Third World is dependent on imports for its weapons; industrialised countries are, for the most part, not,' writes researcher Nicole Ball. 'Third World governments feel they are being discriminated against when arms control proposals deal solely with the transfer of weapons and leave the issue of production untouched.'[12]

Disarmament and development

Nevertheless, several Third World governments *have* launched anti-arms trade initiatives and are clearly concerned about the effect of arms imports and high military spending on development. In fact, as debt and foreign exchange problems bite deeper, many governments may well become increasingly receptive to controls on arms imports and on regional arms races, simply because they can no longer compete with the military shopping lists of neighbouring countries.

Latin America

In 1975, eight Latin American countries – Argentina, Bolivia, Chile, Colombia, Ecuador, Panama, Peru and Venezuela – signed the Declaration of Ayacucho which stated their desire to create conditions permitting effective arms limitation in the region. These countries later held informal meetings of their foreign ministers to explore the possibilities of arriving at an actual commitment in this area. Unfortunately, this declaration was marred by the refusal of Brazil, the leading military power in Latin America, to take part in the discussions.

In July 1985 nineteen Latin American states signed the Declaration of Lima calling for a reduction in military expenditures. It was agreed that the additional funds thus saved should be assigned to the social and economic development of their countries. As a result of this agreement, Peru only bought two Mirage fighter aircraft from France the following year instead of the four previously ordered. This reduction was not simply a unilateral gesture but was taken in the context of dialogues with Chile and Ecuador, Peru's immediate neighbours. It is thought to bear some relation to Peru's extreme problems in servicing its debt, making it very difficult for the Peruvian government to continue purchasing expensive weapons. The government hoped that a regional arms control agreement would discourage neighbouring governments from buying expensive weapons, thereby removing the 'threat' to Peru's security.

A number of Third World governments have submitted proposals for transferring military expenditure to development aid in the Third World. In 1978, for example, President Senghor of Senegal proposed a

5% tax to be imposed internationally on armaments with the resulting funds to be used solely for development assistance. Other proposals have come from Tunisia (1984), Mexico (1984) and Sri Lanka (1985). In 1987, representatives from over a hundred Third World countries were amongst those who attended a UN Special Conference on Disarmament and Development in New York. At this conference, it was primarily the intransigence of western governments which blocked agreement on any concrete steps.

1988 UN Third Special Session on Disarmament

In marked contrast to previous Special Sessions on Disarmament, a wide range of states highlighted the need for openness and restraints in the field of conventional arms transfers. Some 30 states from all political groups urged action on this issue, with many Third World governments claiming that they were being used as testing grounds for new weapons and that, through their arms purchases, they were also subsidising arms industries in the industrialised world. While some Third World delegates emphasised that the arms trade was the responsibility of the *exporter* countries, others claimed that Third World governments also had a duty to help control this trade.

UN General Assembly *(UN photo 172,800/Yutaka Nagata)*

UN THIRD SPECIAL SESSION – THE DEBATES

'*Some Third World countries have become the greedy customers of conventional arms to prosecute protracted wars and have thus unwittingly turned themselves into laboratories for testing weapons produced by developed nations . . . the General Assembly should accord deserving attention to the problems of conventional weapons and their transfer.*' – Oben Asamoah, Secretary for Foreign Affairs, Ghana.

'*. . . Arms merchants continue to exacerbate our conflicts for their own profit. To a considerable extent the developing countries share responsibility for this imbalance. Some fall prey to the overtures of the arms dealers who, in many cases, contribute to creating a false sense of insecurity. Consequently, they devote a disproportionate share of their budgets to military expenditures. We must also be prepared to redress that imbalance by spending less on armaments and more on development.*' – Paul Kawanga Ssemogerere, Minister of Foreign Affairs, Uganda.

'*Military and civilian leaders alike are increasingly asking themselves whether more is really better. Whether the surplus of weaponry in Europe and worldwide really adds anything to our safety. Whether anyone really benefits from remorselessly raising the ante in an endless game of military poker. And not only East and West. The arsenals of war have been growing apace at least as much in the Third World, where they absorb scarce resources, and contribute to keeping the poor poorer. Almost all the tragic casualties of war in the past forty years have been outside NATO and Warsaw Pact areas . . . disarmament is not just for NATO and the Warsaw Pact. It is for all of us.*' – Sir Geoffrey Howe, Secretary of State for Foreign and Commonwealth Affairs, United Kingdom.

'*One of the obstacles impeding settlement of regional conflicts is the intensive transfusion of weapons into zones of increased confrontation. Therefore the Soviet Union favours restrictions on the sales and supplies of conventional arms.*' – Eduard Shevardnaze, Minister of Foreign Affairs, USSR.

Resolution to the 43rd Session of the UN

Taking further some of the ideas put forward to the UN's Third Special Session on Disarmament, Colombia and Costa Rica tabled a draft resolution on the arms trade to the 43rd Session of the United Nations (1988–89). The final version was co-sponsored by some twenty states, including several major arms producers – Britain, West Germany, Italy, Canada and Sweden. The Resolution called on member states to examine on a regional basis ways and means of refraining from acquiring arms additional to those needed for 'legitimate national security'. It also called for more openness around worldwide arms transfers, and for a system enabling member states to report information on arms transfers to the UN. It requested the Secretary-General to 'make available, within the framework of the World Disarmament Campaign, information concerning the question of arms transfers and their consequences for international peace and security.' Finally, the resolution called for the issue of arms transfers to be on the agenda of the 44th Session.

Conclusion

On the whole, attempts to limit transfers of conventional weapons to Third World countries have been either totally unsuccessful or only partially successful. One major problem is that attempts at controlling arms transfers have usually been expressions of vested interests and have had very little to do with the sincere conviction that disarmament would produce positive results. Security is too often thought of in military terms alone, when in fact real security can never be achieved without social and economic stability. Another obstacle in the field of arms trade control is the increasing number of sellers in the market, many of which have few moral scruples. Even when a large number of suppliers implement controls, the multitude of available suppliers usually enables a country to continue purchasing weapons from somewhere. Control and limitations are necessarily the responsibility of governments but governments are not the only force that shapes the arms trade. In recent years the arms trade has become increasingly commercialised and privatised with the result that commercial ambitions often get the upper hand of what would seem to be sound political judgement. Nevertheless, despite all the problems, it is clear that arms transfer limitation is not a dead issue. Many efforts have been made and much can be learnt from them. The increasing concern expressed by *recipient* countries in the Third World is cause for some optimism. It is also encouraging that the issue of arms transfers now has a relatively high profile in the international political agenda.

NOTES

1: See chapter 1.
2: Reported in *Peace and Development* August 1987 produced by Thai Coalition for Peace and Development.
3: Letter sent to CAAT from Ms. Laddawan Tantivitayapitak on 28.12.88.
4: Jose Luiz Goncalves quoted in *Apoio Sindical* no. 1 March 1988 produced by the Metalworkers' Union of Sao Jose dos Campos.
5: Maurilio de Oliveira quoted in AGEN (Agencia Ecumenica de Noticia), Sao Paulo 2.2.89.
6: Unilateral measures were taken against the Chinese Civil War in the 1920s, the Chaco war between Bolivia and Paraguay in 1934, the war between Italy and Ethiopia in 1935.
7: Quote from President Carter's statement on conventional arms transfers on 19 May 1977. For the text of this statement, see US Congress, House Committee on Foreign Affairs, 'Changing Perspectives on US Arms Transfer Policy,' Report by the Congressional Research Service (US Government Printing Office: Washington DC, 1981), pp. 122–123.
8: See Michael T. Klare: 'US policy on Arms Transfers' in *Arms Transfer Limitations and Third World Security* ed. Thomas Ohlson (SIPRI/Oxford University Press 1988).
9: See chapter 10.
10: See chapters 1, 8, and 9 for more information on Britain's interpretation of the UN arms embargo on South Africa.
11: See chapter 9 for more information on British arms sales to Chile.
12: See Nicole Ball: 'Third World Arms Control: a Third World responsibility' in *Arms Transfer Limitations and Third World Security*.